What a treasure our children are, and w<sup></sup>
Christian parents have to raise them to
heart, soul, mind, and strength. With *Se*
Case has served parents well by provi<
biblical, bold, and God-honoring prayer:
behalf of our children. How blessed will
are offered, that our children may indee<

      —BRUCE A. WARE, author of *Big Truths for Young Hearts*
         Professor of Christian Theology
         The Southern Baptist Theological Seminary

Andrew Case has done it again. This time he aids parents in going before
the throne of grace so that we will plead regularly for our children. Using
scripture gives us a new depth of insight into the priorities God wants us to
pray. The preface contains a jewel by W. Scribner, "An Appeal to Parents
to Pray Continually for the Welfare and Salvation of Their Children."
      —TOM & DIANE SCHREINER

There are lots of 'parenting resources' out there for Moms and Dads, on all
kinds of important issues ranging from discipline to talking about sex to
family vacations. One of the most important responsibilities of fathers and
mothers, however, is to pray for and with their children. This book, drawn
mostly right from Holy Scripture, can be a spur to your family to get off the
couch and away from the television and on your knees praying for the
salvation and welfare of your children.
      —RUSSELL D. MOORE, author of *Adopted for Life*
         Senior Vice President
         Southern Baptist Theological Seminary

Our prayer is that God may use this book to motivate parents to pray for
the next generations. The commitment of righteous parents to focused,
purposeful prayer based on God's heart as expressed in His Word "has
great power as it is working" (James 5:16). Use the introduction to inspire
you to pray; and the prayers to inform your mind as you not only agree
with them but also use them as a springboard for your own heartfelt
prayers for your children, grandchildren, and a generation yet unborn.
      —DAVID & SALLY MICHAEL, authors of *Children Desiring God* curricula
         Pastor for Family Discipleship
         Minister for Resources and Program Development
         Bethlehem Baptist Church

Andrew Case has provided parents with a powerful tool: the Word of God turned to prayer—specifically for their children. What a blessing it is to read that prayer is a reminder of our littleness and of God's greatness. That nowhere are we more helpless than in prayer. For it means we can begin where we are, as we are, today.

Soaked in scripture, interspersed with great quotes, this book will encourage, inspire, and strengthen anyone who wants to learn to grow in dependence on God, or—in other words—prayer.

—SALLY LLOYD-JONES
Best-selling author of *The Jesus Storybook Bible*

If we really believe the jaw dropping truth that God uses our prayers to accomplish many of his God glorifying purposes, like the salvation of our beloved children, then O how we should continually ask God to graciously save and preserve them! Andrew Case has encouraged and helped us parents do just this by beautifully putting the treasure of God's Word into prayers for our needy children.

—RANDY & MICHELE MURRAY

As a father, I continually feel inadequate to the task of praying for the three precious children God has entrusted to me. I understand that I need to pray and I genuinely want to pray. Yet I am so often lost when it comes to knowing how. In Setting Their Hope in God, Andrew Case turns to the ultimate prayer book, the Bible, to craft prayers for parents who want to see their children turn to the Lord, to live for the Lord, to honor him with their lives. I am convinced that this book will prove an indispensable resource to many mothers and fathers as they seek to hold up their children before the throne of grace.

—TIM CHALLIES, www.challies.com

We Christian parents, to whom God has committed a holy trust of raising children, are often at a loss for words when it comes to praying for them. We long for their best, but how exactly to say it? And how to avoid the ruts of prayer into which we often fall and flounder? Here, in this fabulous book of prayers, the deepest longings of our hearts for them are expressed and then some. By themselves these prayers are but words—but may they be joined with faith and the Spirit's power, and prove to be truly efficacious! Thank you, Andrew, for this gem.

—MICHAEL A.G. HAYKIN, Professor of Church History and Biblical
Spirituality, The Southern Baptist Theological Seminary
Author of *The Christian Lover* and *The God Who Draws Near*

for
*my starry lyrics of light*
*Corey and Lilly*

Andrew Case, *Setting Their Hope in GOD*
Edited by Joy Hernandez

ISBN 978-14-4953-4042

# Setting Their Hope
*in*

# GOD

## Biblical Intercession
## for Your Children

*He established a testimony in Jacob and appointed a law in Israel,
which He commanded our fathers to teach to their children, that the
next generation might know them, the children yet unborn, and arise
and tell them to their children, so that they should set their hope in God
and not forget the works of God, but keep His commandments.*
~Psalm 78:5-7

# Contents

# Preface

## That Their Hearts May Rejoice in the LORD

Seldom is there more exuberance than that which erupts when a new soul enters the world. When God's son was born Heaven exploded with song (Luke 2:13). Birth is an occasion for saying, "Glory to God in the highest!" It is an occasion for joining the psalmist, singing, "He gives the barren woman a home, making her *the joyous mother of children*. Praise the LORD!" (Ps 113:9). It gives rise to songs like Hannah's: "My heart exults in the LORD; my strength is exalted in the LORD" (I Sam 2:1). There is no question that God takes unbridled delight in creating families. And just as much as through birth, He revels uproariously in building families through adoption. As the apostle Paul writes,

> In love He predestined us *for adoption as sons* through Jesus Christ, according to the purpose of His will, to the praise of His glorious grace, with which He has blessed us in the Beloved. (Eph 1:4-6)

The LORD even chose to use an adopted son as the great leader who would bring His people out of Egypt and mediate His covenant with them (Ex 2:10). And it was the valiance of an adopted daughter that rescued her people from genocide (Esther 2:7). Yahweh glories in this. He glories in the creation of families, no matter how conventional or unconventional, for the sake of His name. Indeed, children are a remarkable gift from the LORD. They are endlessly special and precious to Him. He even tells us that unless we become like them, we will never enter His Kingdom (Matt 18:3).

Do you feel the severe enthusiasm of Heaven? "Behold, children are a *heritage* from the LORD, the fruit of the womb a *reward*" (Ps 127:3).

With such joy comes grave responsibility. All parents have the dark potential to follow the prodigal son in squandering their lavish inheritance and reward (Luke 15:11-32). Their own sin can easily lead to the loss of their children's souls. Terrifying unknowns spread out before our children like minefields scattered with the "passions of the flesh, which wage war against [their souls]" (I Pet 2:11). Still more terrifying is the realization that we, as parents, are ultimately *unable* to save them from the easy way "that leads to destruction" (Matt 7:13). And this forces us to our knees. We must entrust their hearts and paths to the One who not only creates families, but also loves to redeem them.

Thus our duty remains to prayerfully labor and laboriously pray for their salvation and welfare. The parents who neglect this, even while offering their children every other worldly comfort and opportunity, waste their reward and do their children great harm. As William Gurnall wrote,

> Can there be a greater heartache in this life than to see your own child running full speed toward hell, and know that you were the one who outfitted him for the race? Oh, do your best while they are young and in your constant care, to win them to God and set them on the road to heaven.[1]

Care for your sons and daughters wisely, for it is no small undertaking. Indeed, "There's no work more complex, more important, or more exalted that that of caring for children. After all, it's what God Himself has chosen, above all else, to

---

[1] William Gurnall, *The Christian in Complete Armour* (Carlisle: Banner of Truth Trust, 1986), 176.

do with His time."[2] Prayerful labor must include diligent teaching as the LORD requires: "And these words that I command you today shall be on your heart. You shall *teach them diligently to your children*" (Deut 6:6-7). Surely this command was in the psalmist's mind when he prayed, "So even to old age and gray hairs, O God, do not forsake me, until I proclaim Your might to another generation, Your power to all those to come" (Ps 71:18). Likewise, Asaph builds his entire psalm upon the LORD's command to make known His wonders to our children. Listen to his reasoning for singing the history of Yahweh's deeds:

> We will not hide them [the "sayings from of old"] from their children, but tell to the coming generation the glorious deeds of the LORD, and his might, and the wonders that he has done. He established a testimony in Jacob and appointed a law in Israel, which he commanded our fathers to teach to their children, that the next generation might know them, the children yet unborn, and arise and tell them to their children, so that they should set their hope in God and not forget the works of God, but keep his commandments; and that they should not be like their fathers, a stubborn and rebellious generation, a generation whose heart was not steadfast, whose spirit was not faithful to God. (Ps 78:4-8)

Let us likewise make known to our children His faithfulness (Isa 38:19). And let us then fall to our knees and ask that He would use His Word to set their hope in Him. Let us plead importunately that He would never let them forget His works. Let us implore that they would keep His commandments; that they would trust in the power and sufficiency of Christ. In other words, let us pray the Scriptures for our children. O what a treasure trove of prayer is afforded to us in

---

[2] Mike Mason, *The Mystery of Children* (Colorado Springs: WaterBrook, 2001), 51.

the Bible! Seize its wisdom of petition and exultation, and learn to be a conduit of its perfect intercession, committing your sons and daughters to the Father who is gracious, compassionate, and mighty to save (Ps 145:8, 103:13, Isa 63:1). Only by His strength will your children see Him and be glad. Only by His Spirit will their hearts "rejoice in the LORD" (Zech 10:7).

Not until after ten years of wavering prayers did George Mueller learn the value of praying Scripture. What follows is his description of this marvelous discovery.

> The difference then between my former practice and my present one is this. Formerly, when I arose, I began to pray as soon as possible.... But what was the result? I often spent a quarter of an hour, or half an hour, or even an hour on my knees before being conscious to myself of having derived comfort, encouragement, humbling of soul, &c.; and often, after having suffered much from wandering of mind for the first ten minutes, or a quarter of an hour, or even half an hour, I only then began *really to pray*. I scarcely ever suffer now in this way.
>
> My practice had been, at least for ten years previously, as an habitual thing, to give myself to prayer, after having dressed myself in the morning. *Now*...the first thing I did, after having asked in a few words the Lord's blessing upon His precious word, was, to begin to meditate on the word of God, searching, as it were, into every verse, to get blessing out of it.... The result I have found to be almost invariably this, that after a very few minutes my soul has been led to confession, or to thanksgiving, or to intercession, or to supplication; so that, though I did not, as it were, give myself to *prayer*, but to *meditation*, yet it turned almost immediately more or less into prayer. When thus I have been for awhile making confession, or intercession, or supplication, or have given thanks, I go on to the next words or verse, turning all, as I go on, into prayer for myself or others, as the Word may lead to it.[3]

---

[3]George Mueller, *A Narrative of Some of the Lord's Dealing with George Mueller, Written by Himself, Jehovah Magnified. Addresses by George Mueller Complete and Unabridged,* 2 vols. (Muskegon, Mich.: Dust and Ashes Publications, 2003), 1:272-273.

This book is meant to be a help and guide for that kind of praying. It consists of little else than the Word of God turned "more or less into prayer." And more specifically it is a means toward one part of prayer—prayer for the children God has given you. We would do well to heed the council of Thomas Manton: "plead the promise of God in prayer, show Him His handwriting; God is tender of His Word."

### Introducing Precious Past Wisdom

When contemplating a preface for this book I stumbled across a wonderful nugget of parental exhortation and instruction. In its antiquity it shines with pure, gilded wisdom, convicting insight, and biblical practicality. I decided that I could not really improve upon it, so allow me to introduce William Scribner. In 1873 he published a work entitled *An Appeal to Parents to Pray Continually for the Welfare and Salvation of Their Children*. Phil Roberts of Stoke-on-Trent, England kindly gave me permission to use his condensed version of Scribner's arguments. Although I have endeavored to smooth out and update some of the writing, the archaic style can still be a little bumpy at times. Please press on in spite of this. It will be well worth your time and effort.

### An Appeal to Parents to Pray Continually for the Welfare and Salvation of Their Children
by *William Scribner*
(edited by Phil Roberts & Andrew Case)

Although praying for our children is clearly a biblical duty it is too frequently neglected. Often this arises from a secret unbelief regarding the likelihood or possibility of conversion and true religion in childhood and early youth. This has arrested and prevented prayer and effort for this great blessing.

However, the early conversion of all the children of the Church should be intensely desired and incessantly prayed for. Many who are converted only as adults suffer from evil habits developed in their youth. Not only would these be prevented, but habits which none but a true Christian prizes—habits such as daily and systematic prayer, determined fighting with sin in its various forms, generosity, watchfulness over self, and others of a similar kind—are usually formed strongest when young.

In addition, we should expect the conversion of the children of believers as much as, if not more than, others who attend the church and who are not yet believers. Often children are not converted because parents leave their work to others. Valuable though Sunday school teachers are, no parents can be released from the obligation of striving by their own personal efforts to lead their children to Christ. We are commanded to bring our children up "in the discipline and instruction of the Lord" (Eph 6:4). In the case of the children of believers, parental training should be the first and usual means of their salvation. The work to be done by parents includes:

a. Instructing them in the faith.

b. Setting them a holy example.

c. Restraining them.

d. Praying for them.

It is this last aspect which is the focus here.

Praying for Your Children's Salvation

You should pray for your children's conversion because:

1. *Their salvation is so great a prize that it is worth all the pains which your prayer to secure it for them may cost you.*

The fact that their souls are precious beyond all thought, that the loss of their souls would be inconceivably dreadful, that eternal life would be an infinite gain to them, and that your prayers may be instrumental in saving them, should stir you up to offer constant requests on their behalf.

2. *Few will pray for them if you do not.*

Though we are commanded to intercede for all men (1 Tim 2:1), few engage in this duty as they should. When it is done, those who are prayed for are often those who are considered important in the Church's or the world's estimation.

3. *No one else can pray for them as you do.*

The genuine love you have for your children, the tenderness you feel for them, and your knowledge of their makeup, needs, and problems, qualify you to plead with God on their behalf with an urgency and earnestness which can take no refusal. When God wants to convince us of His willingness to hear prayer, He bases His argument on His parental love: "If you then, who are evil, know how to give good gifts to your children, how much more will the heavenly Father give the Holy Spirit to those who ask Him!" (Luke 11:13).

4. *Your omitting to do so will be perilous to them and to you.*

God notes our attempts to fulfill our parental obligations. It is not to unfaithful, prayerless parents that His exceeding great and precious promises are addressed: "But the steadfast love of the LORD is from everlasting to everlasting on those who fear Him, and His righteousness to children's children, to those who keep His covenant and remember to do His commandments" (Ps 103:17-18). Your children are surrounded by evil influences and they are fallen creatures. They need to be protected by the power of God, and no less do they need to be inwardly restrained, enlightened, controlled, purified, and guided by the Holy Spirit.

5. *You will then find it easier to perform other parental duties, which God has ordained as a means to their salvation.*

God commended Abraham for being one who would fulfill his parental duties (Gen 18:19): "For I have chosen him, that he may command his children and his household after him to keep the way of the LORD by doing righteousness and justice, so that the LORD may bring to Abraham what He has promised him." God's will for you as a parent is clear: "And these words that I command you today shall be on your heart. You shall teach them diligently to your children, and shall talk of them when you sit in your house, and when you walk by the way, and when you lie down, and when you rise" (Deut 6:6-7). It is a great work, and nothing can sustain you under the burden like praying for your children, believingly, earnestly, and perseveringly. In giving attention to instruction and discipline, do not neglect prayer! Some blessings seldom come except in answer to heartfelt prayer. One of these is the early conversion of our children.

6. *Prayer alone can call into exercise that divine power on their behalf, which is absolutely necessary in order that the prayers which you may employ for their salvation may not be used in vain.*

Only God's mighty power can effect the great change necessary, raising them to life from a state of spiritual death. Your child is absolutely dependent upon the influences of God's all-powerful Spirit. Though you persevere in the use of means, without the Spirit it will be in vain. Nothing but believing prayer can secure His power to effect the change.

7. *By their salvation, granted in answer to your prayers, your Saviour will be glorified*

Not merely the salvation of your children, but the glory of your dear Saviour in their salvation, should impel you to pray for them. This motive should be stronger than any other which can influence you to seek their salvation.

Praying for Your Children's Welfare
Do not consider only your children's salvation but pray also for your children's welfare because:

1. *You may then expect, as a result of your prayers, that the power of God will counteract in some measure the evil you have done them.*

Even the best of parents sometimes do their children harm. This may be as a result of undue severity in discipline, partiality or injustice, but equally by misguided tenderness and lack of conscientiousness in exercising authority. Unceasing prayer will enable you to avoid these sins. Thoughtful love for them and an earnest desire for their real good would replace mere fondness, and you would be led to avoid the extremes of harshness and hurtful indulgence.

2. *There will be critical periods in their lives when, without your incessant prayers, they my be left to act most unwisely, if not disastrously.*

Pray for them in the momentous decisions concerning matters such as their future career and possible marriage. Do not put off praying over these because they might be in the distant future. Consider, you may not be alive when they face these decisions.

3. *It will lead you to a better understanding of them.*

Fervent prayer, continuously offered for them, in which their special wants, as far as you know them, are spread before God, will be sure to lead to a greater watchfulness over them. It will lead to a closer study of their character and to more exact understanding of their traits and wants. You should know what motives most easily influence them and what temptations are most likely to lead them into wrongdoing. You should also be familiar with their sorrows and circumstances, knowing intimately each one's character. If you are praying for them you will be compelled to note these things.

4. *It will increase your holy desires for them.*

If we cannot pray, even for strangers, without learning to love them, surely the more we commend our children to God, the stronger will our love for their souls become. This steady increase of holy desires in your heart, with reference to your children, will prove an unspeakable blessing both to them and to you.

*5. No other means will be so effectual in enabling you to overcome the difficulty you experience in talking with them on religious subjects.*

Out of the abundance of your heart your mouth will speak. We are often too reserved when it comes to speaking of spiritual matters with our children, despite the scriptural command (Deut 6:7). Nothing is so suited to remove this as earnest, persistent prayer, in which your child's needs are spread before God and specific requests are offered on its behalf.

*6. You will thereby secure for them God's aid in the efforts they may make to yield to you in obedience.*

God requires of children submission to the parent's will and implicit obedience. Children need more than mere human assistance, even though that assistance may come from wise and affectionate parents. They can no more perform their duties as children without such help from God, than you, without such help, can perform your parental duties. You are solemnly bound to think of the dependence of your children on God's help, and earnestly to pray that that help may be given them in their endeavours to honour and obey you.

*7. Other parents seeing your example, may be led to imitate you.*

Others may be challenged by your diligence and may be inspired to be more zealous in their parental duties.

8. *They will often, should they continue in the world, have their times of need when the power of God alone can avail to help them.*

Disappointments, sickness, losses, cares, in short, adversity in various forms, will be sure to overtake them sooner or later, and well will it be for them if you have anticipated these times of need by much prayer offered on their behalf. There will be times of temptation when they will be in fearful danger. The evil one will seek to lay snares for them and at such times earthly friends will be of no help. Ask the Saviour to defend them from the spite, power, and wiles of evil spirits, the agents of Satan who are constantly around them.

In closing, never approach the throne of grace with your own wants without remembering your children's. They are no less helpless and needy than you. Let us resolve that we will give ourselves more intently to the work of interceding for our children. Whether or not we pray for our offspring will decide what our distant descendants are to be, and what kind of influence they will exert. Surely our fervent prayers for God's blessing on our children would be offered without ceasing were we able to fully comprehend the far-reaching results of such prayers.

# Instructions to the Reader

## Make It Your Own

Jesus Christ is emphatically the foundation for every prayer to the Father. But the reader will notice that not all of these prayers put this precious truth into words, simply because they are meant to be springboards that launch us into other specific and more personal prayer. You are encouraged to use them as a means of centering your mind on the Bible, so that what follows in your own individual supplications will be sweetened and guided by the Word and Spirit of God.

Therefore many times I have left it to you, the reader, to be mindful that we pray in Christ's name alone. Indeed, as He Himself said, "No one comes to the Father except through me" (John 14:6). Thus we are to come to the Father in prayer always through Christ and only through Christ. Only because He is our great high priest can we "with confidence draw near to the throne of grace, that we may receive mercy and find grace to help in time of need" (Heb 4:16). And we are to give "thanks always and for everything to God the Father in the name of our Lord Jesus Christ" (Eph 5:20).

While using these prayers, be encouraged to use the names of your children whenever possible. Also, keep in mind that not every part of every prayer will apply to your child(ren). Due to the nature and layout of this particular prayer book, there may be entire prayers or parts of prayers that will not be suitable to pray for an unregenerate child. For example, there are many prayers throughout the book (mostly toward the second half) that praise God for His effectual, saving work that has been made manifest in their hearts. If this has not yet happened in one or some of your children's hearts, you may want to skip over it, or turn it into a prayer that God would indeed save them.

It would be beneficial to pray these prayers with your children often so that they will feel your affection for them, learn how to pray the Scriptures, become more familiar with the Bible, and be reminded of their need for a Savior, Keeper, and Heavenly Father.

Know that if you have only one child you will need to be mindful of the exclusive use of the plural in this book. Also, although some passages have been made gender-inclusive, many still retain the masculine default of the biblical text. This should not be confusing to families with daughters, rather it should only serve to accustom them to the Bible's male tone, which is never intended to be understood as chauvinistic.

When praying with your children, a short exhortation or encouragement for them is often included, usually beginning with "My children..." (John 13:33). Take these as occasions to lift their spirits, to strengthen their souls, to instruct their minds, to gladden their hearts, to put a rock of confidence under their feet, to tenderly and humbly correct, and most of all, to point them to God as their all-satisfying joy.

As with all prayer, these must be employed in a spirit of humility, considering them better and more significant than yourself (Phil 2:3). Be ever conscious of your broken condition—that you are a sinful parent who is in need of continual renewal by which you are being conformed to the image of Christ (Rom 8:29). Therefore pray strongly, as one who knows you are weak. Pray boldly, as one who knows you have no ability or confidence of yourself. Pray sweetly, as one well aware of the heart within you still tinged with the bitter fruit of wickedness. And pray mindful of the truth that you are in need of just as much intercession as they. "This is the one to whom I will look: he who is humble and contrite in spirit and trembles at My word" (Isa 66:2).

Finally, I solemnly charge you before the God and Father of our Lord Jesus Christ to never neglect the joy and privilege of interceding for your children. God has shown marvelous favor to you. "Behold, children are a heritage from the LORD, the fruit of the womb a reward" (Ps 127:3). Therefore pray for them with all your might while you live. Whatever you do for them, do not fail or forget to do the best thing. They are a gift too wonderful for you to care for alone; Sovereign Grace must guard, guide, and govern their hearts and lives.

> If you never enter your closet, and shut the door, if you never plead at the mercy-seat for your child, how can you expect that God will honour you in its conversion?...
> Pray with your children separately, and it will surely be the means of a great blessing. If this cannot be done, at any rate there must be prayer, much prayer, constant prayer, vehement prayer, the kind of prayer which will not take a denial, like Luther's prayer, which he called the bombarding of heaven; that is to say, the planting a cannon at heaven's gates to blow them open, for after this fashion fervent men prevail in prayer; they will not come from the mercy-seat until they can cry with Luther, "*Vici*," "I have conquered, I have gained the blessing for which I strove." "The kingdom of heaven suffereth violence, and the violent take it by force." May we offer such violent, God-constraining, heaven-compelling prayers, and the Lord will not permit us to seek His face in vain![4]

---

[4]Charles Spurgeon, *The Soul Winner* (Grand Rapids: Eerdmans, 1963), 152-53

*Be encouraged, dear Christian reader, with fresh earnestness to give yourself to prayer, if you can only be sure that you ask for things which are for the glory of God.*
~George Mueller

*Prayer, at its best, is the noblest, the sublimest, the most magnificent, and stupendous act that any creature of God can perform on earth or in heaven. Prayer is far too princely a life for most men. It is high, and they are low, and they cannot attain it.*
~Alexander Whyte

Keeper of Your elect,
It is better to take refuge in You than to trust in man. It is better to take refuge in You than to trust in princes. Therefore cause my dear children to take refuge in You alone. Be their strength and their song; be their great salvation.

Let them lift up the cup of salvation and call on Your Name. Open to them the gates of righteousness, that they may enter through them and give thanks to You. Raise their eyes to the hills to see from where their help comes. For their help comes from You, who made heaven and earth. Do not let their feet be moved; keep them and do not slumber. Please keep them and neither slumber nor sleep. Keep them from all evil; keep their lives. Keep their going out and their coming in from this time forth and forevermore.

My children, do you know who keeps you? The LORD is your keeper; the LORD is your shade on your right hand. The sun shall not strike you by day, nor the moon by night.

Lord Jesus, keep my children. We wait eagerly for Your appearing. Hasten the wonderful day of Your return—the wedding supper of the Lamb. Amen (Psalm 118, 116, 121).

recious Provider,

Your testimonies are wonderful; therefore my soul keeps them. May my precious children keep them also. The unfolding of Your word gives light; it imparts understanding to the simple. May they open their mouths and pant, because they long for Your commandments. Turn to them and be gracious to them, as is Your way with those who love Your name.

Keep steady their steps according to Your promise, let no iniquity get dominion over them. Redeem them from man's oppression, that they may keep Your precepts. Make Your face shine upon them, and teach them Your statutes. May their eyes shed streams of tears, because people do not keep Your law (Psalm 119).

*A man cannot live unless he takes his breath, nor can the soul,*
*unless it breathes forth its desires to God.* ~Thomas Watson

LORD God of heaven,

The great and awesome God who keeps covenant and steadfast love with those who love Him and keep His commandments, let Your ear be attentive and Your eyes open, to hear the prayer of Your servant that I now pray before You day and night for my children. Grant them continual patience and forbearance to live with me, a wicked parent. For I have sinned against You; I have acted very corruptly against You by forsaking my responsibility to lead them in righteousness and the fear of You; I have not kept Your commandments, Your statutes, or the rules that You commanded Your servant Moses.

Prevent them from following my old self—when I am unfaithful to Your Word, when I neglect prayer, fail to redeem the time, speak carelessly, walk foolishly, fail to hope in You, seek great things for myself, become anxious about tomorrow. Protect them from my own indwelling sin—when I am beset with the fear of man, the cares of the world, or the love of money. May they never lose confidence that, in spite of my many iniquities and shortcomings, I am Your servant whom You have redeemed by Your great power and by Your strong hand.

O Lord, let Your ear be attentive to the prayer of Your servant. May they delight to fear Your name, and give success to them today, and grant them mercy (Nehemiah 1).

erciful Master,

Look on my children's affliction and deliver them, and let them not forget Your law. Plead their cause and redeem them; give them life according to Your promise! Salvation is far from the wicked, for they do not seek Your statutes. Great is Your mercy, O LORD; give them life according to Your rules.

Even when their persecutors and adversaries are many, let them not swerve from Your testimonies. May they look at the faithless with pity, because they do not keep Your commands. Enable them to love Your precepts! Give them life according to Your steadfast love. The sum of Your word is truth, and every one of Your righteous rules endures forever (Psalm 119).

*To begin the day with prayer is but a formality unless it go on in prayer, unless for the rest of it we pray in deed what we began in word. One has said that while prayer is the day's best beginning it must not be like the handsome title-page of a worthless book. ~ P. T. Forsyth*

overeign Preserver,

Let my dear children stand up and bless You our God from everlasting to everlasting. Blessed be Your glorious name, which is exalted above all blessing and praise. You are the LORD, You alone. You have made *them*. You have made heaven, the heaven of heavens, with all their host, the earth and all that is on it, the seas and all that is in them; and You preserve all of them; and the host of heaven worships You.

Thank You for preserving my children, for keeping them as Your chosen, for directing their steps on the narrow way. Please continue to preserve their lives! For You are the LORD, the God who chose them and brought them out of darkness and made their hearts faithful before You. Thank You that You have kept the promises that are theirs in Christ Jesus, for You are righteous. I praise You that You are a God ready to forgive, gracious and merciful, slow to anger and abounding in steadfast love, and have not departed from them. Even when they stray and their hearts grow dull, You in Your great mercies have not forsaken them. Therefore, keep on making a name for Yourself through them, and instruct them with Your good Spirit. Amen (Nehemiah 9).

hou Great Being who made and rules the world, Put Your Spirit in my children with perfect power that their lives may bear His fruit. May they be loving men and women; joyful and peaceful; patient, kind, and good. Make their souls and actions abound with faithfulness, gentleness, and self-control, for against such things there is no law. By Christ Jesus crucify their flesh with its passions and desires.

Let them not grow weary in doing good, for in due season they will reap if they do not give up. And may they never boast except in the cross of our Lord Jesus Christ, by which the world has been crucified to them, and they to the world (Galatians 5 & 6).

*Prayer seem'd to be natural to me; as the breath, by which the inward burnings of my heart had vent.* ~Jonathan Edwards

reat God,

May my children be inclined to pour themselves out for the hungry and satisfy the desire of the afflicted, so that their light will rise in the darkness and their gloom be as the noonday. Then guide them continually and satisfy their desire in scorched places. Make their bones strong, so that they are like a watered garden, like a spring of water, whose waters do not fail.

May they be radiant; their hearts thrilled to say, "I will greatly rejoice in the LORD; my soul shall exult in my God, for He has clothed me with the garments of salvation; He has covered me with the robe of righteousness." Make them count the garments of salvation as sufficient clothing, valued by them as more precious and worthy of care than the adornments of kings and queens. May their robes of righteousness be ever prevalent, outshining worldly dress. Amen (Isaiah 58 & 61).

ighteous are You, O LORD, and right are Your rules. You have appointed Your testimonies in righteousness and in faithfulness.

Your promise is well tried; may my children love it. Even when they are small and despised, let them not forget Your precepts. Your righteousness is righteous forever, and Your law is true. When trouble and anguish find them out, make Your commandments their delight. Your testimonies are righteous forever; give them understanding that they may live.

With my whole heart I cry for them; answer me, O LORD! Cause them to keep Your statutes. I call to You; save them, that they may observe Your testimonies. I rise before dawn and cry for help; may they hope in Your words. Awaken their eyes before the watches of the night, that they may meditate on Your promise. Hear my voice according to Your steadfast love; O LORD, according to Your justice give them life. When they draw near who persecute them with evil purpose, who are far from Your law, assure them that You are near, O LORD, and all Your commandments are true. Long have I known from Your testimonies that You have founded them forever (Psalm 119).

*What makes a heart upright and what makes prayers pleasing to God is a felt awareness of our tremendous need for mercy.*
~John Piper

y Gracious Master,

Cause my delightful children to work out their own salvation with fear and trembling, knowing all the while that it is You who work in them, both to will and to work for Your good pleasure.

May they rejoice in You always, and let their reasonableness be known to everyone. Please let them not be anxious about anything, but in everything by prayer and supplication with thanksgiving may they make known their requests to You. Please do this so that Your peace, which surpasses all understanding, will guard their precious hearts and minds in Christ Jesus.

Finally Father, make them think on whatever is true, whatever is honorable, whatever is just, whatever is pure, whatever is lovely, whatever is commendable, on anything of excellence, and anything worthy of praise. Through Your Son and for Your glory I ask these things. Amen (Philippians 2 & 4).

eavenly Father,

As for me, my prayer is to You. At an acceptable time, O God, in the abundance of Your steadfast love answer me in Your saving faithfulness. And my prayer is this: deliver my children from sinking in the mire of sin; let them be delivered from the deep waters of vanity. Let not the flood sweep over them, or the deep swallow them up, or the pit of despair close its mouth over them. Answer me, O LORD, for Your steadfast love is good; according to Your abundant mercy turn to them. Draw near to their soul, redeem them; ransom them because of their frailty.

When they are afflicted and in pain, let Your salvation, O God, set them on high! Then may they praise Your Name with a song, and magnify You with thanksgiving. May they seek You, and rejoice and be glad in You!

My children, because we love His salvation, let us say together evermore, "God is great!" Hasten to us, O God! You are our help and our deliverer; O LORD, do not delay! Save us for Your marvelous Name (Psalm 69 & 70).

lessed God,

Although princes may persecute them without cause, may my precious children's hearts stand in awe of Your words. Might they, by the power of Your Spirit, rejoice at Your word like one who finds great spoil. Make them hate and abhor falsehood, but love Your law. Cause them to praise You seven times a day for Your righteous rules. Great peace have those who love Your law; nothing can make them stumble. May they hope for Your salvation, O LORD, and do Your commandments. Cause their souls to keep Your testimonies and love them exceedingly. Help them to keep Your precepts and testimonies, for all their ways are before You.

Let my cry come before You, O LORD; give them understanding according to Your word! Let my plea come before You; deliver them according to Your word. May their lips pour forth praise, for You teach them Your statutes. May their tongues sing of Your word, for all Your commandments are right. Let Your hand be ready to help them, and may they choose Your precepts. Create in them a longing for Your salvation, O LORD, and a delight in Your law. Let their souls live and praise You, and let Your rules help them. When they go astray like lost sheep, seek them, and do not let them forget Your commandments. Amen (Psalm 119).

*You often feel that your prayers scarcely reach the ceiling; but, oh, get into this humble spirit by considering how good the Lord is, and how evil you all are, and then prayer will mount on wings of faith to heaven. The sigh, the groan of a broken heart, will soon go through the ceiling up to heaven, aye, into the very bosom of God.* ~Charles Simeon

*Even skeptical Dan prayed, his skepticism falling away from him like a discarded garment in this valley of the shadow, which sifts out hearts and tries souls, until we all, grown-up or children, realize our weakness, and, finding that our own puny strength is as a reed shaken in the wind, creep back humbly to the God we have vainly dreamed we could do without.*
~L.M. Montgomery

ord Jesus,

It is by Your undying death and willing sacrifice that I come to my Father who has loved me with an everlasting love for His own purpose and glory. And so I ask, LORD and Sovereign, that my children would be blessed because their ways are blameless; that they would walk in the law of the LORD! Cause them to keep Your testimonies and seek You with their whole hearts, doing no wrong but walking in Your ways.

May they keep Your precepts diligently for love of Your great Name. Oh, that their ways may be steadfast in keeping Your statutes! May their eyes be fixed unswervingly on all Your commandments. Please ignite such joy in them that they must praise You with upright hearts when they learn Your righteous rules. And cause them to keep Your statutes; do not utterly forsake them!

Keep their way pure by teaching them to guard it according to Your word. Make them into such men and women who seek You with their whole hearts, crying out, "Let me not wander from Your commandments." May they store up Your word in their hearts that they might not sin against You. Blessed are You, O LORD; teach them Your statutes!

May their lips be consecrated to declaring the rules of Your mouth. My plea is that in the way of Your testimonies they would delight as much as in all riches...as much as in all friends...more so than any worldly lust and pleasure. Quicken their minds to meditate on Your precepts and fix their eyes on Your ways. Let them delight in Your statutes and not forget Your word (Psalm 119).

*How much my father's prayers at this time impressed me I can never explain, nor could any stranger understand. When, on his knees and all of us kneeling around him in Family Worship, he poured out his whole soul with tears for the conversion of the Heathen world to the service of Jesus, and for every personal and domestic need, we all felt as if in the presence of the living Savior, and learned to know and love him as our Divine friend.*
~John G. Paton

neffable Lover,

Only by the Cross do I bring these prayers to You for my treasured daughters. Do not let their adorning be merely external—the braiding of hair, the wearing of gold, or the putting on of clothing—but let their adorning be the hidden person of the heart with the imperishable beauty of a gentle and quiet spirit, which in Your sight is very precious.

Give all my children unity of mind, sympathy, brotherly love, a tender heart, and humility. The end of all things is at hand; therefore let them be self-controlled and sober-minded for the sake of their prayers. Above all, keep them loving others earnestly, since love covers a multitude of sins.

As they have received gifts, may they use them to serve others, as good stewards of Your varied grace. When they speak, let it be as those who speak the oracles of God; when they serve, as one who serves by the strength that You supply—in order that in everything You may be glorified through Jesus Christ. To You belong glory and dominion forever and ever. Amen (I Peter 3 & 4).

od of my end,

Deal bountifully with my children that they may live and keep Your word. And this I ask with importunate reverence: open their eyes, that they may behold wondrous things out of Your law. O that their eyes would sparkle with pure and deep delight when Your Truth is shone into them out of grace. For they are mere sojourners on this earth; hide not Your commandments from them!

Consume their souls with longing for Your rules at all times, for You rebuke the insolent, accursed ones, who wander from Your commandments. Take away from them scorn and contempt, for they have kept Your testimonies. Cause them to meditate on Your statutes even when princes sit plotting against them. May their lips be ready to say, "Your testimonies are my delight; they are my counselors."

When their souls cling to the dust please give them life according to Your word! When they tell You of their ways, answer them; teach them Your statutes! Make them understand the way of Your precepts and meditate on Your wondrous works.

When their souls melt away for sorrow—for they *will* be well-acquainted with grief if they are Yours—strengthen them according to Your word! They are ever surrounded by false ways in this age; teach them Your law! They have chosen the way of faithfulness; may they set Your rules ever before them. When they cling to Your testimonies, O LORD, let them not be put to shame! Enlarge their hearts so that they may run in the way of Your commandments! (Psalm 119).

*How easily we convince ourselves that we are praying to the Lord when in reality we are locked in our own thoughts. We need to ask: If I'm happy, am I really rejoicing in Him, or am I rejoicing in my own self-satisfaction? If I'm worried or afraid, am I truly and humbly asking Him for help, or is my mind busy trying to work out some plan (however spiritual it may seem) for getting myself out of trouble.* ~Mike Mason

lmighty God,
Please teach my wonderful children the way of Your statutes; may they keep it to the end, as their reward. Give them understanding that they may keep Your law and observe it with their whole hearts. Lead them in the path of Your commandments, because they delight in it—O Father, cause them to delight in Your path!

Incline their hearts to Your testimonies, and not to selfish gain! Turn their eyes from looking at worthless things; and give them life in Your ways. Confirm to them Your promise, that they may fear You. Turn away the reproach that they dread, for Your rules are good. Behold, may they long for Your precepts; in Your righteousness give them life!

Let Your steadfast love come to them, O LORD, Your salvation according to Your promise; then shall they have an answer for anyone who taunts them, for they trust in Your word. Sovereign LORD, may they trust the Bible with all their might! And take not the word of truth utterly out of their mouths, for their hope is in Your rules. May they keep Your law continually, forever and ever, and may they walk in a wide place, for they have sought Your precepts.

Make them also speak of Your testimonies before kings and not be put to shame, for they find their delight in Your commandments, which they love. May they lift up their hands toward Your commandments, and meditate on Your statutes. Amen, come Lord Jesus (Psalm 119).

ather of Wisdom,

Let me never cease to pray for my children, asking that they may be filled with the knowledge of Your will in all spiritual wisdom and understanding, so as to walk in a manner worthy of You, bearing fruit in every good work and increasing in the knowledge of You. May they be strengthened with all power, according to Your glorious might, for all endurance and patience with joy, giving thanks to You, who have qualified them to share in the inheritance of the saints in light.

Do you remember, my children, that He has delivered you from the domain of darkness and transferred you to the kingdom of His beloved Son, in whom you have redemption, the forgiveness of sin? Yes, praise Him with me for His marvelous grace!

O LORD God, make them continue in the faith, stable and steadfast, not shifting from the hope of the gospel that they heard, which has been proclaimed in all creation under heaven. Keep them! Keep them! Keep them in the love of Christ. Amen (Colossians 1).

*Anyone who would have power in prayer must be merciless in dealing with his own sins.* ~R.A. Torrey

iver of all,

Remember Your word to Your servant, in which You have made me hope. May my children's comfort in their affliction be this: that Your promise gives them life. The insolent might utterly deride them, but do not let them turn away from Your law. When they think of Your rules from of old, let them take comfort, O Lord. O that hot indignation might seize them because of the wicked, who forsake Your law. And I ask that Your statutes would be their songs in the house of their sojourning. Cause them to remember Your Name in the night, O Lord, and keep Your law. This blessing has fallen to them, that they have kept Your precepts.

When they kneel to pray, let them say, "You are my portion; I promise to keep Your words." I entreat Your favor with all my heart; be gracious to them according to Your promise. When they think on their ways, let them turn their feet to Your testimonies; may they hasten and not delay to keep Your commandments. Though the cords of the wicked ensnare them, allow them not to forget Your law. And this I plead with fervent hope—that at midnight they would rise to praise You, because of Your righteous rules, for only by a miracle of Your hand will it be so with them. Make them the companions of all who fear You, of those who keep Your precepts. The earth, O Lord, is full of Your steadfast love; teach them Your statutes! (Psalm 119).

God,

Blessed are those who fear You, who greatly delight in Your commandments! Please continue to mold my children into such men and women.

Make light dawn in the darkness for them; You are gracious, merciful, and righteous. Grant that they deal generously and lend, conducting their affairs with justice. Let them never be moved; remember them forever.

May they be not afraid of bad news, but make their hearts firm, trusting in You. Give them steady hearts, so that from the rising of the sun to its setting they will praise Your glorious Name.

My children, trust in the LORD! He is your help and your shield. I admonish you again, my children, trust in the LORD! He is your help and your shield. You who fear the LORD, trust in Him! He is your help and your shield. May you be blessed by the LORD, who made heaven and earth! We will bless You, O God, from this time forth and forevermore. Praise the LORD! (Psalm 112, 113, 115).

*We are not so foolish as to think we can learn a trade without the diligent use of helps. Shall we think that we may become spiritually skilful and wise in the understanding of this mystery without making any real effort to use the helps God has given us? The most important of them is fervent prayer. Pray with Paul that 'the eyes of your understanding may be enlightened to behold' the glory of God in Christ. Pray that the 'God of our Lord Jesus Christ, the Father of glory, may give to you the spirit of wisdom and revelation in the knowledge of him.' Fill your minds with spiritual thoughts of Christ. Lazy souls do not get the tiniest sight of this glory. The 'lion in the way' deters them from making the slightest effort.* ~John Owen

Great Upholder and Proprietor of all things, Please deal with my children according to Your word. Teach them good judgment and knowledge, for they believe Your commandments. Even though they have gone astray before their affliction, assist them now to keep Your word. You are good and do good; teach them Your statutes. Although the insolent may smear them with lies, help them keep Your precepts with their whole hearts; the insolent's heart is unfeeling, but my children delight in Your law.

It is good for them to be afflicted, that they might learn Your statutes. And if this be what sanctifies them further, please bring suffering to them again. May the law of Your mouth be better to them than thousands of gold and silver pieces. Your hands have made and fashioned them; give them understanding that they may learn Your commandments. May those who fear You see them and rejoice, because they have hoped in Your word. I know, O LORD, that Your rules are righteous, and that in faithfulness You afflict them. Let Your steadfast love comfort them according to Your promise to Your servant.

Let Your mercy go to them, that they may live; and make Your law their delight. Let the insolent be put to shame, because they have wronged them with falsehood; as for them, may they meditate on Your precepts. Let those who fear You turn to them, that they may know Your testimonies. May their hearts be blameless in Your statutes, that they may not be put to shame! Amen (Psalm 119).

timeless Light of lights, Eternal Father, Make my children's souls long for Your salvation; may they hope in Your word. Be the cause of their eyes longing for Your promise; of their asking, "When will You comfort me?" Let them seek the deepest of comfort in Your steadfast love and faithfulness. When they become like a wineskin in the smoke, let them not forget Your statutes. How long must Your servant endure? When will You judge those who persecute them? The insolent have dug pitfalls for them; they do not live according to Your law. All Your commandments are sure; they persecute my children with falsehood; help them! When they have almost made an end of them on earth, let my children not forsake Your precepts. In Your steadfast love give them life, that they may keep the testimonies of Your mouth.

Forever, O LORD, Your word is firmly fixed in the heavens. Your faithfulness endures to all generations; You have established the earth and it stands fast. By Your appointment they stand this day, for all things are Your servants. If Your law is not made to be my children's delight, they will surely perish in their affliction. Oh, that they would never forget Your precepts, for by them You have given them life. They are Yours, save them, for they have sought Your precepts. When the wicked lie in wait to destroy them, may they consider Your testimonies. I have seen a limit to all perfection, but Your commandment is exceedingly broad. Give them life in Your ways. Amen. Come, Lord Jesus (Psalm 119).

*It is very apparent from the word of God, that he is wont often to try the faith and patience of his people, when crying to him for some great and important mercy, by withholding the mercy sought, for a season; and not only so, but at first to cause an increase of dark appearances. And yet he, without fail, at last succeeds those who continue instant in prayer, with all perseverance, and will not let him go except he blesses.*
~Jonathan Edwards

hangeless God,

May my children never forget all Your benefits.

Help me to remind them relentlessly of the One who forgives all their iniquity, who heals all their diseases, who redeems their lives from the pit, who crowns them with steadfast love and mercy, who satisfies them with good so that their youth is renewed like the eagle's.

Please work righteousness and justice for them when they are oppressed. Make known Your ways to them, Your acts to Your precious children.

O gifts of heaven, hear again of our marvelous God! The LORD is merciful and gracious, slow to anger and abounding in steadfast love. He will not always chide, nor will He keep His anger forever. He does not deal with you according to your sins, nor repay you according to your iniquities. For as high as the heavens are above the earth, so great is His steadfast love toward those who fear Him; as far as the east is from the west, so far does He remove your transgressions from you.

O LORD, as a father shows compassion to his children, please show compassion to them. For You know their frame; You remember that they are dust.

Come quickly, Lord Jesus! Amen, we long and wait for You (Psalm 103).

*There is nothing in which we need to take so many lessons as in prayer. There is nothing of which we are so utterly ignorant when we first begin; there is nothing in which we are so helpless. ~Alexander Whyte*

overeign Creator and Sustainer,

Oh how I love Your law! May it be my children's meditation all the day. Your commandment makes them wiser than their enemies, for it is ever with them. Grant them more understanding than all their teachers by making Your testimonies their meditation. May they understand more than the aged, because they keep Your precepts. Assist them to hold back their feet from every evil way, in order to keep Your word. May they not turn aside from Your rules, for You have taught them. Please cause them to say, "How sweet are Your words to my taste, sweeter than honey to my mouth!" Through Your precepts make them get understanding, and so hate every false way.

May Your word be a lamp to their feet and a light to their path. May they swear an oath and confirm it, to keep Your righteous rules. When they are severely afflicted please give them life, O LORD, according to Your word! Accept their free offerings of praise, O LORD, and teach them Your rules. Though they may hold their lives in their hands continually, let them not forget Your law. When the wicked lay a snare for them, may they not stray from Your precepts. Make Your testimonies their heritage forever, and the joy of their hearts. Incline their hearts to perform Your statutes forever, to the end. Amen (Psalm 119).

weet Sustainer and Rock of Salvation, I do not ask that You take my dear children out of the world, but that You keep them from the evil one. Sanctify them in the truth; Your word is truth. Father, I desire that they also, whom You have given to Christ, may be with Him where He is, to see His glory that You have given Him because You loved Him before the foundation of the world.

I give thanks to You always for my children because of Your grace that has been given them in Christ Jesus, and I ask that in every way they may be enriched in You in all speech and all knowledge—even that the testimony about Christ might be confirmed in them—so that they will not be lacking in any spiritual gift, as they wait for the revealing of our Lord Jesus Christ, who will sustain them to the end, guiltless in the day of Christ.

O God, be the source of their lives in Christ Jesus, whom You made their wisdom and their righteousness and sanctification and redemption. Therefore, let them boast solely in You. For the display of Your wonderful winsomeness, Amen (John 17 & I Corinthians 1).

*Desire gives fervor to prayer. The soul cannot be listless when some great desire fixes and inflames it...Strong desires make strong prayers...The neglect of prayer is the fearful token of dead spiritual desires...There can be no true praying without desire.* ~E. M. Bounds

Father of my dearest Lord Jesus,
May my children hate the double-minded, but love Your law. Be their hiding place, and their shield; make them hope in Your word. Cause evildoers to depart from them, that they may keep the commandments of their God. Uphold them according to Your promise, that they may live, and let them not be put to shame in their hope! Hold them up, that they may be safe and have regard for Your statutes continually! You spurn all who go astray from Your statutes, for their cunning is in vain. All the wicked of the earth You discard like dross, therefore may my children love Your testimonies. Might they say in their hearts, "My flesh trembles for fear of You, and I am afraid of Your judgments."

They have done what is just and right; do not leave them to their oppressors. Give them a pledge of good; let not the insolent oppress them. May their eyes long for Your salvation and for the fulfillment of Your righteous promise. Deal with my children according to Your steadfast love, and teach them Your statutes. Make them Your servants; give them understanding, that they may know Your testimonies! It is time for You to act, for Your law has been broken. Therefore, may they cry in their hearts, "I love Your commandments above gold, above fine gold. Therefore I consider all Your precepts to be right; I hate every false way." Amen.

Come Lord Jesus (Psalm 119).

ur Father in heaven, Hallowed be Your Name. Please keep Your Name holy in the lives of my children. Cause them to consider it reverently in their minds and hearts, treating it as sacred by their words and conduct.

May Your kingdom come, and may they long for the day of Your fullness far more than anything else in this life. Stir their hearts to seek first Your kingdom.

Your will be done on earth as it is in heaven. Perform Your good pleasure in them—use them as vessels to magnify the beauty of Your Son. Give them this day their daily bread, providing for their physical needs, for You are a loving, merciful Father who gives good gifts to His children. Teach them to trust You, being not anxious about whether they will have enough for tomorrow.

Forgive them their debts, as they also forgive their debtors. Forgive them when they fall short of Your glory. And form in them pardoning hearts, forbearing in everything.

Lead them not into temptation, but deliver them from evil. Rescue them from the deceitfulness of sin. By Your undeserved mercy keep their hearts from being darkened and led into foolishness. For Yours is the kingdom, the power, and the glory forever! Amen (Matthew 6).

*Giving God good advice, and abusing the devil isn't praying.*
~L.M. Montgomery

y Exceeding Joy,

Help me never to cease giving thanks for my dear children, remembering them in my prayers, that You, the God of my Lord Jesus Christ, the Father of glory, may give them a spirit of wisdom and of revelation in the knowledge of You, having the eyes of their hearts enlightened, that they may know what is the hope to which You have called them, what are the riches of Your glorious inheritance in the saints, and what is the immeasurable greatness of Your power toward us who believe, according to the working of Your great might.

O LORD, they cannot know and delight in the mystery and beauty of Your gospel unless Your Spirit intervenes, bringing about fruit in them for righteousness. For this reason I bow my knees before You, Father, from whom every family in heaven and on earth is named, that according to the riches of Your glory You may strengthen them with power through Your Spirit in their inner beings, so that Christ may dwell in their hearts through faith—that they, being rooted and grounded in love, may have strength to comprehend with all the saints what is the breadth and length and height and depth, and to *know* the love of Christ that surpasses knowledge, that they may be filled with all of Your fullness.

Now to You who are able to do far more abundantly than all that we ask or think, according to the power at work within us, to You be glory in the church and in Christ Jesus throughout all generations, forever and ever Amen (Ephesians 1 & 3).

erciful LORD,
I know that it is Your good pleasure to give of Yourself to those who ask; therefore I pray that my precious children's delight would be in Your law. May they meditate on it day and night. Teach them what it is to serve You with fear and rejoice with trembling.

O LORD, be a shield about them, their glory, and the lifter of their heads. Assist them to put their trust in You so that their hearts exult, saying, "You have put more joy in my heart than they have when their grain and wine abound." In peace make them both lie down and sleep; for You alone, O LORD, make them dwell in safety. Lead them, O LORD, in Your righteousness because of their enemies; make Your way straight before them. Let them take refuge in You and rejoice; let them ever sing for joy, and spread Your protection over them, that they who love Your Name may exult in You.

For You bless the righteous, O LORD; You cover them with favor as with a shield. May they give to You the thanks due to Your righteousness, and sing praise to Your Name, Most High.

My children, give thanks to the LORD with your whole heart; recount all of His wonderful deeds! Be glad and exult in God; sing praise to His Name, the Most High. For those who know Your Name, O LORD, put their trust in You, for You have not forsaken those who seek You.

Remind them that they are but dust, wholly dependent upon You for life and breath and everything else. I commit them to You. Amen (Psalm 2, 4, 5, 9).

hou Great I Am,
You are righteous; You love righteous deeds; the upright shall behold Your face. Therefore cause my children to walk uprightly so that they might do what they were made for—behold Your wonderful face! May they trust in Your steadfast love; may their hearts rejoice in Your salvation. And then let them sing to You, because You have dealt bountifully with them. Again I ask that they be constrained to walk blamelessly and do what is right and speak the truth in their hearts.

O that they would say and continue to say to You, "You are my Lord; I have no good apart from You. You are my chosen portion and my cup; You hold my lot." May they set You always before them; trusting that because You are at their right hand, they shall not be shaken. Please make known to them the path of life; that in Your presence there is fullness of joy; at Your right hand are pleasures evermore.

Wondrously show Your steadfast love to them, O Savior of those who seek refuge from their adversaries at Your right hand. Keep them as the apple of Your eye; hide them in the shadow of Your wings. May they behold Your face in righteousness; when they awake, may they be satisfied with Your likeness. Praise the LORD! (Psalm 11, 13, 16, 17).

*No prayer is more powerful than
the prayer of powerlessness, of littleness, of not knowing.
Isn't this what it means to be poor in spirit?* ~Mike Mason

triune God,

I love You, O LORD, my strength. May You be to my children their rock and their fortress and their deliverer, their God, their rock, in whom they take refuge, their shield, and the horn of their salvation, their stronghold. You alone are worthy to be praised.

By Your mercy bring them out into a broad place; rescue them, because You delight in them. Put all Your rules before them, and may they never put Your statutes away from them. For it is You who light their lamps; O LORD my God, lighten their darkness. Make them abide in this precious promise: "This God—His way is perfect; the word of the LORD proves true; He is a shield for all those who take refuge in Him."

Give them the shield of Your salvation, and with Your right hand support them, and with Your gentleness make them great. With Your perfect law, O LORD, revive their souls. With Your sure testimony make them wise. By Your right precepts cause their hearts to rejoice. And may Your pure commandment enlighten their eyes.

Keep them also from presumptuous sins; let them not have dominion over them! Let the words of their mouths and the meditation of their hearts be pleasing in Your sight, O LORD, my Rock and my Redeemer (Psalm 18 & 19).

nfinite Father,

It is my plea by the Name of Christ, that You hear me on behalf of my sweet children. Since they are of Your holy and beloved chosen, then put on them compassion, kindness, humility, meekness, and patience. And if one has a complaint against them, let them forgive as You have forgiven them. And above all these put on them love, which binds everything together in perfect harmony.

And let the peace of Christ rule in their hearts, to which indeed they were called. And may they be thankful. Let the word of Christ dwell in them richly, as they admonish others in all wisdom, singing psalms and hymns and spiritual songs, with thankfulness in their hearts to You. And whatever they do, in word or deed, may everything be in the Name of the Lord Jesus, giving thanks to You, their Father, through Him.

My children, continue steadfastly in prayer, being watchful in it with thanksgiving. I commit you to our dearest and fairest Lord Jesus. He will sustain you. Amen (Colossians 3 & 4).

ll-sufficient King,

    May You answer my dear children in the day of trouble! May Your great Name, God of Jacob, protect them! Grant their hearts' desire and fulfill all their plans! May they shout for joy over Your salvation, and in the name of their God set up their banners! May You fulfill all their petitions.

Some trust in chariots and some in horses, but let *them* trust in the name of the LORD their God. Make them glad with the joy of Your presence. Be exalted, O LORD, in Your strength! Let them sing and praise Your power.

When trouble is near and there is none to help, be not far from them. For You, O LORD, are their Shepherd; they shall not want. Please make them to lie down in green pastures. Lead them beside still waters. Restore their souls. And by grace, lead them in paths of righteousness for Your Name's sake.

Even when they walk through the valley of the shadow of death, let them fear no evil, for You are with them; with Your rod and Your staff comfort them. May goodness and mercy follow them all the days of their lives, that they may dwell in Your house forever (Psalm 20 & 23).

*For my part, if I cannot pray, I would rather know it, and groan over my soul's barrenness till the Lord shall again visit me with fruitfulness of devotion.* ~Charles Spurgeon

ife-giving God,

O that the children You have provided for me would have clean hands and a pure heart! Guard them so that they do not lift up their souls to what is false or swear deceitfully. Guide them so that they might receive blessings from You and righteousness from the God of their salvation. Cause them to seek You, to seek the face of the God of Jacob.

To You, O Lord, I lift up their souls. O my God, in You I trust; let them not be put to shame; let not their enemies exult over them. Make them to know Your ways, O Lord; teach them Your paths. Lead them in Your truth and teach them, for You are the God of their salvation; for You they wait all the day long.

According to Your steadfast love remember them, for the sake of Your goodness, O Lord! Lead them in humility and what is right; teach them Your way. Instruct them in the way You should choose.

Your friendship, O Lord, is for those who fear You, and You make known to them Your covenant. And so I ask importunately that You would fill them with the fear of You so that they might be Your friends.

Cause their eyes to be ever toward You. Turn to them and be gracious to them when they are lonely and afflicted. O guard their souls and deliver them! Let them not be put to shame, for they take refuge in You. May integrity and up-rightness preserve them, for they wait for You (Psalm 24 & 25).

ord of Heaven,

Cause my children to walk in integrity. May they trust in You without wavering. Prove them, O LORD, and try them; test their hearts and their minds. Manifest Your steadfast love before their eyes that they may walk in Your faithfulness. Redeem them and be gracious to them.

You are their light and their salvation; whom shall they fear? You are the stronghold of their life; of whom shall they be afraid?

O LORD, I love how You have made them Your habitation and a place where Your glory dwells. I pray that they would earnestly say with the Psalmist, "One thing have I asked of the LORD, that will I seek after: that I may dwell in the house of the LORD all the days of my life, to gaze upon the beauty of the LORD and to inquire in his temple."

Let their hearts also cry, "Your face, LORD, do I seek." Hide not Your face from them. Cast them not off; forsake them not, O God of my salvation!

My children, wait for the LORD; be strong, and let your hearts take courage; wait for the LORD! (Psalm 26 & 27).

*Prayer often avails where everything else fails.* ~R.A. Torrey overeign Commander of the universe, You are my children's only true strength and shield; in You may their hearts trust and be helped; let their hearts exult, and with their songs give thanks to You. You are the strength of Your people; be the saving refuge of my precious children. May You give strength to them!

When they are mourning, turn it into dancing; loose their sackcloth and clothe them with gladness, that their glory may sing Your praise and not be silent. O LORD my God, I will give thanks to You forever!

In You, O LORD, may they take refuge; let them never be put to shame; in Your righteousness deliver them! Cause them to rejoice and be glad in Your steadfast love. Make Your face shine on them; save them in Your steadfast love!

O my beloved earthly treasures, the LORD preserves the faithful; be strong and let your hearts take courage, you who wait for the LORD!

Keep them, Father; I commit them wholly to Your Hand (Psalm 28, 30, 31).

Fountain of all good,
Instruct my cherished children and teach them in the way they should go; counsel them with Your eye upon them.

May Your steadfast love surround them because they trust in You. Make them glad in You; make them rejoice as the righteous, shouting for joy as the upright in heart!

Let all the earth fear the LORD; let all the inhabitants of the world stand in awe of You! For You spoke, and they came to be; You commanded, and they stand firm. Behold, how good it is that Your eye is on those who fear You, on those who hope in Your steadfast love. O that their souls would wait for You; be their help and their shield. Together, may our hearts be glad in You, because we trust in Your holy Name. Let Your steadfast love, O LORD, be upon us, even as we hope in You.

Cause them to bless You at all times; may Your praise continually be in their mouths. Let them say, "My soul makes its boast in the LORD; let the humble hear and be glad."

Dearest children, oh magnify the LORD with me, and let us exalt His Name together! (Psalm 32, 33, 34).

*There is a general kind of praying which fails for lack of precision. It is as if a regiment of soldiers should all fire off their guns anywhere. Possibly somebody would be killed, but the majority of the enemy would be missed.* ~Charles Spurgeon

earcher of hearts,

I ask with reverent joy and trembling that my children would taste and see that You are good! Blessed are those who take refuge in You! Be near to them when they are brokenhearted, saving them when they are crushed in spirit.

Say to their souls, "I am your salvation!" Then their souls will rejoice in You, exulting in Your salvation. May all their bones say, "O LORD, who is like You, delivering the poor from him who is too strong for him, the poor and needy from him who robs him?"

You have seen, O LORD; be not silent! O Lord, be not far from them! Then their tongues shall tell of Your righteousness and of Your praise all the day long.

Make them feast on the abundance of Your house, and give them drink from the river of Your delights. For with You is the fountain of life; in Your light do we see light. O continue Your steadfast love toward them, and Your righteousness to the upright of heart! Let not the foot of arrogance come upon them, nor the hand of the wicked drive them away.

Please fill them with grace daily, that their lives might be a fountains of sweet water. Amen (Psalm 34, 35, 36).

O God who hears the prayers of Your children, Only You can bring my children to trust in You and do good; to dwell in the land and befriend faithfulness. Only Your Hand can turn their hearts like a stream of water to delight themselves in You so that You will give them the desires of their hearts.

My children, listen to my entreaty: commit your way to the LORD; trust in Him, and He will act. He will bring forth your righteousness as the light, and your justice as the noonday.

Father, let them be still before You and wait patiently for You, not fretting themselves over the one who prospers in his way, over the man who carries out evil devices. For their steps are established by You, when You delight in their way; though they fall, they will not be cast headlong, for You uphold their hands.

It is my humble plea that their souls would take hope in Your words through David: "I have been young, and now am old, yet I have not seen the righteous forsaken or their children begging for bread."

May their mouths utter wisdom, and their tongues speak justice. May the law of their God be in their hearts so that their steps do not slip (Psalm 37).

*Necessity!—I hardly like to talk of that, let me rather speak of the deliciousness of prayer—the wondrous sweetness and divine felicity which come to the soul that lives in the atmosphere of prayer. John Fox said, "The time we spend with God in secret is the sweetest time, and the best improved. Therefore, if thou lovest thy life, be in love with prayer." The devout Mr. Hervey resolved on the bed of sickness—"If God shall spare my life, I will read less and pray more." John Cooke, of Maidenhead, wrote—"The business, the pleasure, the honour, and advantage of prayer press on my spirit with increasing force every day." A deceased pastor when drawing near his end, exclaimed, "I wish I had prayed more"; that wish many of us might utter.*
~Charles Spurgeon

ORD of the cloud and fire,

The salvation of my children is from You; You are their stronghold in the time of trouble. You help them and deliver them; please deliver them from the wicked and save them, because they take refuge in You.

Do not forsake them, O LORD! O my God, be not far from them! Make haste to help them, O Lord, my salvation!

O LORD, make them know their end and what is the measure of their days; let them know how fleeting they are! Behold, You have made their days a few handbreadths, and their lifetimes are as nothing before You. Surely all mankind stands as a mere breath!

Hear my prayer—may they wait patiently for You; incline to them and their cries. Draw them up from the pit of destruction, out of the miry bog, and set their feet upon a rock, making their steps secure. Put a new song in their mouths, a song of praise to their God. May many see them and fear, and put their trust in You.

Blessed is the man who makes the LORD his trust. As for You, O LORD, do not restrain Your mercy from them; Your steadfast love and Your faithfulness will ever preserve them!

My children, hope in God! Amen (Psalm 37, 39, 40).

God most high, most glorious, Be pleased to deliver my children! O LORD, make haste to help them! Let those be put to shame and disappointed altogether who seek to snatch away their lives.

But may they seek You and rejoice and be glad in You; may they love Your salvation and say continually, "Great is the LORD!" You are their help and their deliverer; do not delay, O my God!

As the deer pants for flowing streams, so may their souls pant for You. May their souls thirst for God, for the living God.

When their souls are cast down and in turmoil within them, let them hope in You and praise You—their salvation and their God. By day You command Your steadfast love, and at night may Your song be with them, a prayer to the God of their lives.

Send out Your light and Your truth; let them lead them; let them bring them to Your dwelling! Then take them to Your altar; let them delight in You as their exceeding joy and praise You with the lyre, O God, my God.

Why are you cast down, my children, and why are your souls in turmoil within you? Hope in God; for He is worthy of praise, your salvation and your God! (Psalm 40, 42, 43).

*Only he who is himself secure and happy in the Lord can pray effectively for others.* ~Mike Mason

lector of Saints,

May my dear children boast continually in You, and give thanks to Your Name forever. Please redeem them for the sake of Your steadfast love! Be their refuge and strength, a very present help in trouble. Therefore we will not fear though the earth gives way, though the mountains be moved into the heart of the sea.

O God, be near them so that they will not be moved; help them when morning dawns. Make them to be still and know that You are God. And then let them clap them hands, shouting to You with loud songs of joy!

Know, my children, that the LORD, the Most High, is to be feared, a great king over all the earth. Sing praises to God, sing praises! Sing praises to our King, sing praises! For God is the King of all the earth; sing praises with a psalm!

Cause them to think on Your steadfast love, O God. Your praise reaches to the ends of the earth. Your right hand is filled with righteousness. Let them be glad! Let my children rejoice because of Your judgments!

Ransom their souls from the power of Sheol, and out of them shine forth.

My children, shine forth the shimmering beauty of our Lord Christ! Amen (Psalm 46, 47, 48, 49).

Living God,

Incline my children's hearts to offer You a sacrifice of thanksgiving. Have mercy on them according to Your steadfast love; according to Your abundant mercy blot out their transgressions. Wash them thoroughly from their iniquity, and cleanse them from their sin! Make them know their transgressions and in humility have their sin ever before them.

Purge them with hyssop, and they shall be clean; wash them, and they shall be whiter than snow. Let them hear joy and gladness; let the bones that You have broken rejoice. Hide Your face from their sins, and blot out all their iniquities. Create in them clean hearts, O God, and renew right spirits within them.

Cast them not away from Your presence, and take not Your Holy Spirit from them. Most of all I pray, *restore unto them the joy of Your salvation*, and uphold them with willing spirits. Then their tongues will sing aloud of Your righteousness. O Lord, open their lips, so that their mouths will declare Your praise.

O my gifts of heaven, the sacrifices of God are a broken spirit; a broken and contrite heart He will not despise (Psalm 50 & 51).

⊛

*Why are we called "adulteresses" in praying for something to spend on our pleasures? Because God is our husband and the "world" is a prostitute luring us to give affections to her that belong only to God. This is how subtle the sin of worldliness can be. It can emerge not against prayer, but in prayer—and fasting. We begin to pray and fast—even intensely—not for God as our all-satisfying husband, but only for his gifts in the world so that we can make love with them.* ~John Piper

oly LORD,

Make my treasured children trust in Your steadfast love forever and ever. May they thank You forever, because You are saving them. O that they would wait for Your Name, for it is good.

Save them, by Your Name, and vindicate them by Your might. O God, hear my prayer; give ear to the words of my mouth. Hide not Yourself from my plea for mercy! Sustain them as they cast their burdens upon You; when they are afraid let them trust in You.

In You, whose word we praise, in You we trust; we shall not be afraid. What can flesh do to us? This we know, that You are *for* us.

My children, do not be afraid, for what can man do to you? God is *for* you! You need not fear.

Deliver their souls from death, yes, their feet from falling, that they may walk before You in the light of life. Be merciful to them, O God, be merciful to them, for in You their souls take refuge; in the shadow of Your wings let them take refuge, till the storms of destruction pass by.

Fulfill Your purpose for them and be exalted above the heavens. Let Your glory be over all the earth!

Dearest children, sing and make melody with me! We give thanks to You, O Lord, among the peoples; we will sing praises to You among the nations. For Your steadfast love is great to the heavens, Your faithfulness to the clouds (Psalm 52, 54, 56, 57).

Changeless God,
Deliver my priceless children from their enemies; protect them from those who rise up against them. Then they shall sing of Your strength; make them sing aloud of Your steadfast love in the morning. For You have been to them a fortress and a refuge in the day of their distress. O my Strength, we will sing praises to You, for You, O God, are our fortress, the God who shows us steadfast love.

Hear my cry, listen to their prayer; from the end of the earth may they call to You when their heart is faint. Lead them to the rock that is higher than they, for You are a refuge, a strong tower against the enemy. Let them dwell in Your tent forever! Let them take refuge under the shelter of Your wings! Appoint steadfast love and faithfulness to watch over them!

May they wait for You alone in silence; from You comes salvation. You alone must be their rock and their salvation, their fortress; let them not be greatly shaken. Their hope must come from You.

Trust in Him at all times, my children; pour out your heart before Him; God is a refuge for us (Psalm 59, 61, 62).

y Father,

May my wonderful children earnestly seek You; might their souls thirst for You; make their flesh faint for You, as in a dry and weary land where there is no water. Let them look upon You continually, beholding Your power and glory. And because they know that Your steadfast love is better than life, may their lips praise You.

Form them into men and women who will bless You as long as they live, lifting up their hands in Your Name. Satisfy their souls as with fat and rich food. And I ask that they remember You even upon their beds, and meditate on You in the watches of the night, their mouths praising You with joyful lips. For You have been their help; therefore in the shadow of Your wings let them sing for joy.

My children, let your souls cling to God, for His right hand upholds you! (Psalm 63).

*How, then, do you pray? Do you ask God for your daily bread? Do you thank God for your conversion? Do you pray for the conversion of others? If the answer is 'no', I can only say that I do not think you are yet born again. But if the answer is 'yes'— well, that proves that, whatever side you may have taken in debates on this question in the past, in your heart you believe in the sovereignty of God no less firmly than anyone else. On our feet we may have arguments about it, but on our knees we are all agreed. ~J.I. Packer*

ord and King,
Let my children rejoice in You and take refuge in You! Let their upright hearts exult! Praise is due to You, O God—You who hear prayers. Blessed is the one You choose and bring near, to dwell in Your courts! Please secure their place among such chosen.

Shout for joy to God, my children; sing the glory of His Name; give to Him glorious praise! Say to God, "How awesome are Your deeds! So great is Your power that Your enemies come cringing to You. All the earth worships You and sings praises to You; they sing praises to Your Name."

May they rejoice in You, who rule by Your might forever. Test them and try them as silver is tried. Please, please do not reject their prayer or remove Your steadfast love from them! Instead be gracious to them and bless them and make Your face shine upon them, that Your way may be known on earth, Your saving power among all the nations. May they be glad, exulting before You, jubilant with joy! (Psalm 64, 66, 68).

od of Grace,

Make my children sure of this: that You who began a good work in them will bring it to completion at the day of Christ Jesus. For You alone are my witness, how I yearn for them with the affection of Christ Jesus, and when I do not, assist me to yearn for them as I ought. It is my prayer that their love may abound more and more, with knowledge and all discernment, so that they may approve what is excellent, and so be pure and blameless for the day of Christ, filled with the fruit of righteousness that comes through Jesus Christ, to the glory and praise of Your name.

With special grace I ask that You would enable them to count whatever gain they have as loss for the sake of Christ. Indeed, make them count everything as loss because of the surpassing worth of knowing Christ Jesus their Lord. May they suffer along with me the loss of all things and count them as rubbish, in order that they may gain Christ and be found in Him, not having a righteousness of their own that comes from the law, but that which comes through faith in Christ, the righteousness from You that depends on faith— that they may *know* Christ and the power of His resurrection, and may share in His sufferings, becoming like Him in His death (Philippians 1 & 3).

lmighty God,

Be to my dear children a rock of refuge, to which they may continually come. For You, O Lord, are their hope.

May their mouths be filled with Your praise, and with Your glory all the day. O God, be not far from them; O my God, make haste to help them! May they hope continually and praise You yet more and more. Let their mouths tell of Your righteous acts, of Your deeds of salvation all the day, for their number is past knowledge.

So even to old age and gray hairs, O God, do not forsake them, until they proclaim Your might to another generation, Your power to all those to come (Psalm 71).

*Among all the formative influences which go to make up a man honoured of God in the ministry, I know of none more mighty than his own familiarity with the mercy-seat. All that a college course can do for a student is coarse and external compared with the spiritual and delicate refinement obtained by communion with God. While the unformed minister is revolving upon the wheel of preparation, prayer is the tool of the great potter by which he moulds the vessel. All our libraries and studies are mere emptiness compared with our closets. We grow, we wax mighty, we prevail in private prayer.*
~Charles Spurgeon

lessed be the LORD, the God of Israel,
who alone does wondrous things.

Blessed be Your glorious Name forever; may the whole earth be filled with Your glory!

I come before You with this petition: that my children would be continually with You—may You hold their right hand. Guide them with Your counsel, for it is perfect, wise, and good.

Cause these miraculous, marvelous words to pour from their souls: "Whom have I in heaven but You? And there is nothing on earth that I desire besides You." I know that their hearts and their flesh may fail, therefore be the strength of their hearts and their portion forever.

As for my children, it is good for them to be near You; let them make You their refuge, that they may tell of all Your works. Continue to mold them into men and women who fear You, for who can stand before You once Your anger is roused?

My children, remember the deeds of the LORD; yes, remember His wonders of old. Ponder all His work, and meditate on His mighty deeds.

Your way, O God, is holy. What god is great like our God? You are the God who works wonders; You have made known Your might among the peoples. O please work wonders on their behalf, and with Your arm redeem them (Psalm 72, 73, 76, 77).

od of peace,

It is my request that my children would set their hope in You and not forget Your works, but keep Your commandments. Let them not be like this stubborn and rebellious generation, a generation whose heart is not steadfast, whose spirit is not faithful to You. Make their hearts steadfast toward You and faithful to Your covenant. Thank You for being compassionate and not destroying them; You restrained Your anger from them and did not stir up all Your wrath.

Remember that they are but flesh, a wind that passes and comes not again. Restore them, O God of hosts; let Your face shine, that they may be saved!

My children, call to Him who alone is your salvation! With all your might seek His wonderful, matchless face! (Psalm 78 & 80).

*God has designed not only that prayer come to be, but that prayer sometimes be a necessary means for accomplishing the ends he has ordained. In other words, God purposely designed how things would work so that some of what he accomplishes can only be accomplished as people pray.* ~Bruce Ware

lessed Father,

My children need to need You. O that their souls would long, yes, faint for Your courts; that their hearts and flesh would sing for joy to You, the living God. Give them thankful hearts, ever singing Your praise! Bless them with grateful souls, exalting Your Name forever.

O treasured children, sing aloud to God your strength; shout for joy to the God of Jacob! Raise a song; sound the tambourine, the sweet lyre with the harp.

LORD God of hosts, hear my prayer; give ear, O God of Jacob! Bring them into Your presence, for a day in Your courts is better than a thousand elsewhere. May they rather be a doorkeeper in Your house than dwell in the tents of wickedness.

Be their sun and their shield; bestow on them favor and honor. Withhold no good thing from them, because they walk uprightly. O LORD of hosts, blessed is the one who trusts in You! (Psalm 84).

Thou Giving God,

Be gracious to my wonderful children, for to You do I cry all the day. Gladden the soul of Your servant, for to You, O Lord, do I lift up their souls.

Teach them Your way that they may walk in Your truth; unite their hearts to fear Your Name. Turn to them and be gracious to them; give them strength, and save them.

My children, sing with me of the steadfast love of the LORD forever; with your mouths make known His faithfulness to all generations!

Make them walk in the light of Your face, exulting in Your Name all the day, exalted in Your righteousness. Teach them to number their days that they may get hearts of wisdom. Satisfy them in the morning with Your steadfast love, that they may rejoice and be glad all their days. Make them glad for the days You have afflicted them, and for as many years as they have seen evil. Let Your work be shown to them, and Your glorious power to their children. Amen (Psalm 86 & 89).

lorious God,
Let Your favor be upon my sweet children. Establish the work of their hands.

Be their dwelling place, Most High, and be their refuge, so that no evil shall be allowed to befall them. Command Your angels concerning them to guard them in all their ways. Because You hold fast to them in love, please deliver them; protect them because they know Your Name.

When they call to You, answer them; be with them in trouble; rescue them and honor them. With long life satisfy them, and show them Your salvation. Satisfy them with Your beauty.

Hear, my children, while I admonish you! Listen to me: there shall be no strange god before you; you shall not bow down to a foreign god. Go to the LORD! Open your mouths wide, and He will fill them. He will feed you with the finest of wheat, and with honey from the rock He will satisfy you (Psalm 90, 91, 81).

*Prayer is the process of crouching down and making ourselves small before God. This downsizing is not an option; it is the only way to enter the kingdom of heaven. To grow in the Spirit is to become little in relation to more and more areas of life—marriage, family, church, work—until eventually it is possible to be little and childlike even in the presence of Satan and all his demons. For it is God, not you or I, who is bigger than evil.*
~Mike Mason

aithful Creator,

May grace and peace be multiplied to my matchless children in the knowledge of You and of Jesus our Lord. May they grow in the grace and knowledge of our Lord and Savior Jesus Christ. When they suffer according to Your will, let them entrust their souls to a faithful Creator while doing good.

Let them not love the world or the things in the world, and may they keep themselves from idols.

My children, do not love what is passing away more than your God! Instead build yourselves up in your most holy faith; pray in the Holy Spirit; keep yourselves in the love of God, waiting for the mercy of our Lord Jesus Christ that leads to eternal life.

Now to Him who is able to keep you from stumbling and to present you blameless before the presence of His glory with great joy, to the only God, our Savior, through Jesus Christ our Lord, be glory, majesty, dominion, and authority, before all time and now and forever. Amen (II Peter 3, I John 2, Jude).

lorious and Holy God,

You have made me glad by Your work; at the works of Your hands I sing for joy. How great are Your works, O LORD, for You have made my beautiful children! Your thoughts are very deep! Therefore keep them in Your care, and discipline them, and teach them out of Your law. For blessed are the ones whom You discipline, to give them rest from days of trouble. Do not forsake them or abandon them as Your heritage.

If You are not their help, their souls would soon live in the land of silence. When their feet slip, hold them up, O LORD, with Your steadfast love. When the cares of their hearts are many, cheer their souls with Your consolations. Become their stronghold, and their rock of refuge.

Oh come, my children, and let us sing to the LORD; let us make a joyful noise to the rock of our salvation! Let us come into His presence with thanksgiving; let us make a joyful noise to Him with songs of praise! For You, O LORD, are a great God, and a great King above all gods (Psalm 92, 94, 95).

*If we do not learn to pray, it will not be for want of instructions and examples. Look at Abraham, taking it upon him to speak unto the Lord for Sodom. Look at Isaac, who goes out to meditate in the field at the eventide. Look at Jacob, as he wrestles until the breaking of the day at the Jabbok. Look at Hannah, as she speaks in her heart. Look at David, as he prevents now the dawning of the day, and now the watches of the night, in a hundred psalms. Look at our Lord. And then, look at Paul, as great in prayer as he is in preaching, or in writing Epistles. No, –if you never learn to pray, it will not be for want of the clearest instructions, and the most shining examples.*
~Alexander Whyte

ord Christ,
Only by Your blood and imputed righteous-ness do I approach the Father with confidence concerning my priceless children.

Therefore, Father, as they received Christ Jesus the Lord, may they so walk in Him, rooted and built up in Him and established in the faith, just as they were taught, abounding in thanksgiving.

My children, if then you have been raised with Christ, seek the things that are above, where Christ is, seated at the right hand of God. Set your minds on things that are above, not on things that are on earth. For you have died, and your life is hidden with Christ in God.

Father, help them to walk in their new selves, which are being renewed in knowledge after the image of their Creator. Assist them to put to death what is earthly in them: sexual immorality, impurity, passion, evil desire, and covetousness, which is idolatry. Let them put them all away: anger, wrath, malice, slander, and obscene talk from their mouths. You are the great healer and refiner. Purify my wonderful children by whatever means are necessary. Make them wholly Yours. Amen (Colossians 2 & 3).

ORD God Almighty,

Grant that my children declare Your glory among the nations; Your marvelous works among all the peoples. For great are You LORD, and greatly to be praised; You are to be feared above all gods. Splendor and majesty are before You; strength and beauty are in Your sanctuary.

May my children ascribe to You glory and strength! Let them ascribe to You the glory due Your Name, worshiping You in the splendor of holiness. Make them say among the nations, "The LORD reigns!"

Let them hear of Your righteousness and be glad, rejoicing with the sons and daughters of Judah because of Your judgments, O LORD. May they hate evil, for You preserve the lives of Your saints; You deliver them from the hand of the wicked.

My children come, let us worship and bow down; let us kneel before the LORD, our Maker! For He is our God, and we are the people of His pasture, and the sheep of His hand (Psalm 96 & 95).

*Resolved, never to count that a prayer, nor to let that pass as a prayer, nor that as a petition of a prayer, which is so made, that I cannot hope that God will answer it; nor that as a confession, which I cannot hope God will accept.*
~Jonathan Edwards

ternal Father,

With Your right hand and Your holy arm please work salvation for my dearest children. Remember Your steadfast love and faithfulness to them so that all the ends of the earth will see the salvation of their God.

Make a joyful noise to the LORD, my children; break forth into joyous song and sing praises! Join with the sea as it roars, with the world and those who dwell in it, with the rivers as they clap their hands, with the hills singing for joy together before the LORD.

O God, may they ponder the way that is blameless, and walk in integrity of heart. Let them not set before their eyes anything that is worthless, keeping a perverse heart far from them.

Do not hide Your face from them in the day of their distress! Incline Your ear to them; answer speedily when they call! And by Your infinite mercy grant their hearts to pour forth in song, "Bless the LORD, O my soul, and all that is within me, bless His holy Name" (Psalm 98, 102, 103).

*It is crucial that we not be more fascinated, more gripped, by the prayers of a man than by the pleasures of God. How easy it is to be more thrilled by radical devotion than by divine beauty.*
~John Piper

less the LORD, O my soul! O LORD my God, You are very great! You are clothed with splendor and majesty, covering Yourself with light as with a garment. And by the blood and mercy of Your perfect Son I appeal to Your wise power on behalf of my children.

May their meditations be pleasing to You, for they rejoice in You. Let them thank You for Your steadfast love, for Your wondrous works to the children of men! Satisfy their longing souls; when their souls hunger fill them with good things. Send out Your word and heal them, and deliver them from destruction. Let them sing and make melody with all their being!

Awake, my children! Let us awake the dawn! Give thanks with me to the LORD among the peoples; we will sing praises to Him among the nations. For Your steadfast love, O God, is above the heavens; Your faithfulness reaches to the clouds. Be exalted, O God, above the heavens! Let Your glory be over my children! Amen (Psalm 104, 107, 108).

Lord,
Grant my children help against the foe, for vain is the salvation of man! With You they shall do valiantly. O GOD my Lord, deal on their behalf for Your Name's sake; because Your steadfast love is good, deliver them! With their mouths let them give great thanks to You, praising You in the midst of sorrow. For You stand at the right hand of the needy, to save them from those who condemn their souls to death.

Praise be to You, LORD! I will give thanks to You with my whole heart, in the company of the upright, in the congregation. Great are Your works, studied by all who delight in them. Therefore help me to study my children diligently, for they are Your wonderful handiwork.

Show them the power of Your works—that they are faithful and just; all Your precepts are trustworthy; they are established forever and ever, to be performed with faithfulness and uprightness.

My children, fear the LORD, for it is the beginning of wisdom; all those who practice this fear have a good understanding. His praise endures forever! (Psalm 108, 109, 111).

Divine Comforter,
When my dear children sow in tears, let them reap with shouts of joy. Grant them assurance in the God of their salvation, hoping in You and Your steadfast love.

May they wait for You, and hope in Your word. Continually make them into men and women whose souls wait for You more than watchmen for the morning.

My children, hope in the LORD! For with the LORD there is steadfast love, and with Him is plentiful redemption. Hope in the LORD from this time forth and forevermore.

O God, Your blessing be upon them! I bless them in the Name of the LORD!

I praise You, LORD, for You are good; I sing to Your Name for it is pleasant! Please choose my children for Yourself; make them Your own possession. Do as You please with them; deal with them according to Your sovereign purpose. For I know that You are great, and that You are above all gods (Psalm 126, 130, 128, 135).

*True religion makes us want to spend time alone in meditation and prayer. We read that this was true for Isaac (Gen. 24:63). Even more important, we read in the Gospels that Christ too needed to be alone with His Father. Concealing deep feeling is difficult, and yet grace-filled feeling is often more silent and private than that which is counterfeit.* ~Jonathan Edwards

iving God,

Remember my wonderful children even in their low estate, for Your steadfast love endures forever. Though they walk in the midst of trouble, preserve their lives; stretch out Your hand against the wrath of their enemies and deliver them. Please fulfill Your purposes for them; Your steadfast love, O LORD, endures forever. Do not forsake the work of Your hands.

O LORD, search them and know them! Hem them in, behind and before, and lay Your hand upon them.

I praise You, for they are fearfully and wonderfully made. Wonderful are Your works; my soul knows it very well. Their frames were not hidden from You, when they were being made in secret, intricately woven in the depths of the earth. Your eyes saw their unformed substance; in Your book were written the days that were formed for them, when as yet there were none of them.

Therefore take confidence, my children! The Almighty LORD of heaven and earth will accomplish for you what is best as His children. Faint not; be not downcast but sleep in His gracious providence, for when you awake He is still with you (Psalm 138 & 139).

*I myself have seen this rare beauty on the face of a young woman at prayer, one who most likely had no idea that she was being seen by human eyes. Her countenance was incomparably more lovely than anything Hollywood's cosmetology is able to achieve. Indeed, divine grace working in a receptive soul does produce what St. Paul calls "God's work of art" (Eph 2:10).*
~Thomas Dubay

uthor of Salvation,

Being affectionately desirous of my children, make me ready to share with them not only the gospel of God but also my own self, because they have become very dear to me. Now may You and the Lord Jesus direct their way, and make them increase and abound in love for all, so that You may establish their hearts blameless in holiness before Yourself at the coming of our Lord Jesus with all His saints.

To this end I also pray for them: that You may make them worthy of Your calling and may fulfill every resolve for good and every work of faith by Your power, so that the Name of our Lord Jesus may be glorified in them, and them in Him, according to Your grace and the grace of the Lord Jesus Christ.

I ought always to give thanks to You for them, because You chose them to be saved, through sanctification by the Spirit and belief in the truth.

My children, to this He called you through the gospel, so that you may obtain the glory of our Lord Jesus Christ. So then, stand firm and hold to the traditions that you were taught by His word.

Now may the Lord Jesus Christ Himself, and You, Father, who loved them and gave them eternal comfort and good hope through grace, comfort their hearts and establish them in every good work and word. Amen (I Thessalonians 3 & II Thessalonians 1 & 2).

od of hosts,

Restore my children; let Your face shine, that they may be saved! Search them, O God, and know their hearts! Try them and know their thoughts! And see if there be any grievous way in them, and lead them in the way everlasting!

Set a guard, O LORD, over their mouths; keep watch over the door of their lips! Do not let their hearts incline to any evil, to busy themselves with wicked deeds. Let a righteous word strike them—it is a kindness; let it rebuke them—it is oil for their heads; let their heads not refuse it.

May they cry out to You, O LORD and say, "You are my refuge, my portion in the land of the living." Attend to their cry, especially when they are brought very low.

Cause them to remember the days of old, meditate on all that You have done, and ponder the work of Your hands. Let them stretch out their hands to You when their souls thirst for You like a parched land. Hide not Your face from them, lest they be like those who go down to the pit.

Let them hear in the morning of Your steadfast love, for in You they trust. Make them know the way they should go, for to You I lift up their souls. Amen (Psalm 80, 141, 142, 143).

adiant Redeemer,

Teach them to do Your will, for You are their God! Let Your good Spirit lead them on level ground! For Your Name's sake, O LORD, preserve their lives! In Your righteousness bring their souls out of trouble.

I confess that they and I deserve none of these mercies, but only death and wrath. For what is man that You regard him, or the son of man that You think of him? Man is like a breath; his days are like a passing shadow. But praise be to You, Christ Jesus, for Your righteous obedience and perfect atonement.

My children, do you know His greatness? He is great and greatly to be praised, and His greatness is unsearchable. Extol Him as Your God and King. Every day bless Him and praise His name forever and ever.

Grant, Lord God, that they be men and women who meditate on the glorious splendor of Your majesty and on Your wondrous works. May they speak of the might of Your awesome deeds, and declare Your greatness. Let them pour forth the fame of Your abundant goodness and sing aloud of Your righteousness. Amen (Psalm 143, 144, 145).

*The magnificence of God is the source and measure of the magnificence of prayer. "Think magnificently of God."*
~Alexander Whyte

ing of Kings,

I appeal to Your testimony concerning Yourself: that You are gracious and merciful, slow to anger and abounding in steadfast love. You are good to all, and Your mercy is over all that You have made. Therefore, be eternally kind towards my dear children. Keep them in the love of Christ, and let them give thanks to You and bless You always.

May they speak of the glory of Your kingdom and tell of Your power. Let them make known to the children of man Your mighty deeds, and the glorious splendor of Your kingdom. For Your kingdom is an everlasting kingdom, and Your dominion endures throughout all generations.

My children, *know* this God! He is righteous in all His ways and kind in all His works. Trust this God, for He is near to all who call on Him, to all who call on Him in truth. Love this God, for He fulfills the desire of those who fear Him, and preserves all who love Him.

Let their mouths speak Your praise, O LORD, and let all flesh bless Your holy Name forever and ever (Psalm 145).

*In our Lord's prayer, he told us to pray, "Your kingdom come, your will be done, on earth as it is in heaven" (Matt. 6:10). This indicates that the perfect will of God precedes my praying and yours. We are not told to pray, "your will be* formed," *but "your will be* done." ~Bruce Ware

rince of Peace,

Let my children praise You as long as they live; let them sing praises to their God while they have being. Let them be glad in their Maker, rejoicing in their King! Let them praise Your Name with dancing, making melody to You with their voices. Please take pleasure in their songs and adorn them with salvation.

Let them exult in glory; let them sing for joy on their beds. Let Your high praises be in their throats and Your word in their hands. May they praise You in Your sanctuary; praise You in Your mighty heavens! Make them praise You for Your mighty deeds; praise You according to Your excellent greatness!

Put not your trust in princes, my children, in a son of man, in whom there is no salvation. But blessed are they whose help is the God of Jacob, whose hope is in the LORD their God, who made heaven and earth, the sea, and all that is in them, who keeps faith forever; who executes justice for the oppressed, who gives food to the hungry.

Everything that has breath praise the LORD! Praise the LORD! (Psalm 146, 149, 150).

ise Counselor.

I ask that my children would hear Your instruction and not forsake Your teaching, for they are a graceful garland for their heads and pendants for their necks. All good things come from You, O God, therefore make their ears attentive to wisdom and incline their hearts to understanding; yes, let them call out for insight and raise their voices for understanding, seeking it like silver and searching for it as for hidden treasures. Give them such fervor so that they might understand the fear of You and find the knowledge of God.

Let not steadfast love and faithfulness forsake them; bind them around their necks; write them on the tablet of their hearts.

Trust in the LORD with all your heart, my children! And lean not on your own understanding. In all your ways acknowledge Him, and He will make straight your paths. Be not wise in your own eyes; fear the LORD, and turn away from evil.

Lord God, may they honor You with their wealth and with the firstfruits of all their produce; then their barns will be filled with plenty, and their vats will be bursting with wine. Let them not despise Your discipline or be weary of Your reproof, for You reprove those whom You love, as a father the sons in whom he delights (Proverbs 1, 2, 3, 5).

<hr />

*Better be somewhat too bold and somewhat unseemly than altogether to neglect and forget Almighty God. Better say that so bold saying, —"I will not let Thee go," than pray with such laziness and sleepiness and stupidity as we now pray.*
~Alexander Whyte

ather of our Lord Jesus,
May You direct the hearts of my children to Your love and to the steadfastness of Christ. Work this miracle of grace in them: that they would count it all joy when they meet trials of various kinds.

If they lack wisdom, let them ask You, who give generously to all without reproach, so that it will be given them. Cause them to be doers of the word, and not hearers only, deceiving themselves.

Though they have not seen You, let them love You. Though they do not now see You, let them believe in You and rejoice with joy that is inexpressible and filled with glory, obtaining the outcome of their faith, the salvation of their souls.

May they be part of Your chosen race, Your royal priesthood, Your holy nation, a people for Your own possession, that they may proclaim the excellencies of You who call men out of darkness into Your marvelous light.

To You alone, Lord God, be glory forever! Amen (James 1 & I Peter 1 & 2).

od of Truth,

Please be my children's confidence, and keep their feet from being caught. May they keep hold of instruction and not let it go; let them guard it, for it is their life. Make them commit their work to You so that their plans may be established.

My children, better is a little with the fear of the LORD than great treasure and trouble with it. The fear of the LORD is a fountain of life, that you may turn away from the snares of death.

Father, importunately I ask that they would find wisdom and get understanding, for the gain from it is better than gain from silver and its profit better than gold. May they consider wisdom as more precious than jewels, for long life is in her right hand; in her left hand are riches and honor. Let them not lose sight of these—sound wisdom and discretion, for they will be life for their souls and adornment for their necks (Proverbs 3, 16, 15).

*There is no true prayer without agony. Perhaps this is the problem in many of our churches. What little prayer we have is shallow, timid, carefully censored, and full of oratorical flourishes and hot air. There is little agony in it, and therefore little honesty or humility. We seem to think that the Lord is like everyone else we know, and that He cannot handle real honesty. So we put on our Sunday best to visit Him, and when we return home and take off our fancy duds we are left alone with what is underneath: the dirty underwear of hypocrisy. ~Mike Mason*

ord and Father,

Thank You for calling my dear children to belong to Jesus Christ. I praise You for loving them and calling them to be among the saints!

Grant that we may be mutually encouraged by each other's faith. And let them never be ashamed of the gospel, for it is the power of God for salvation to everyone who believes. For in it Your righteousness is revealed from faith for faith.

Indeed, when they were outside of Christ they failed to please You; they could not. They were not righteous, and there was no fear of You before their eyes.

My children, remember that you have sinned and fallen short of His glory, and are justified by His grace as a gift, through the redemption that is in Christ Jesus, whom God put forward as a propitiation by His blood. And this was to show His righteousness, so that He might be just and the justifier of the one who has faith in Jesus.

Therefore they cannot boast, O LORD, for all that they have is of grace through Christ! May they live and breathe and eat and drink by grace alone, for Your glory alone (Romans 1 & 3).

*God has made the spread of his fame hang on the preaching of his Word; and he has made the preaching of his Word hang on the prayers of the saints. This is the awesome place of prayer in the purposes of God for the world. The triumph of the Word will not come without prayer.* ~John Piper

ncomparable God,

Let my children not continue in sin so that grace may abound. May it never be! Do not allow them to live in sin once they have died to it. Cause them to consider themselves dead to sin and alive to You in Christ Jesus. Let not sin reign in their mortal bodies, to make them obey their passions. Keep them from presenting their members to sin as instruments for unrighteousness. For sin will have no dominion over them, since they are not under law but under grace.

Just as they once presented their members as slaves to impurity and to lawlessness leading to more lawlessness, so now may they present their members as slaves to righteousness leading to sanctification. Instill this truth ever deeply within them: the wages of sin is death, but Your free gift is eternal life in Christ Jesus our Lord. Restrain them from earning deadly wages. And come quickly, Lord Jesus. We long for You. Amen (Romans 5 & 6).

eliciously Gracious Master,

When my children find themselves divided in their desires, help them. Help them when they delight in Your law in their inner being, but they see in their members another law waging war against the law of their minds and making them captive to the law of sin that dwells in their members. And when they cry, "Wretched man that I am! Who will deliver me from this body of death?" make them hope in You through Jesus Christ their Lord!

My children, it is my joy to remind you that there is therefore now no condemnation for those who are in Christ Jesus. For the law of the Spirit of life sets you free in Christ Jesus from the law of sin and death.

O God, cause them to exult in the knowledge that You have done what the law, weakened by the flesh, could not do. By sending Your own Son in the likeness of sinful flesh and for sin, You condemned sin in the flesh, in order that the righteous requirement of the law might be fulfilled in us who walk not according to the flesh but according to the Spirit. Although their bodies are dead because of sin, give them life by the Spirit because of righteousness! Amen (Romans 7 & 8).

*Pray often, for prayer is a shield to the soul,*
*a sacrifice to God, and a scourge for Satan.* ~John Bunyan

lmighty Infinite Father,

If You are for my beloved children, who can be against them? You who did not spare Your own Son but gave Him up for us all, how will You not also with Him graciously give them all things? Who shall bring any charge against them as Your elect? It is You who justify. Who is to condemn? Assure them with the truth that Christ Jesus is the one who died—more than that, who was raised—who is at Your right hand, who indeed is interceding for them. I praise You that no one shall separate them from the love of Christ. Even tribulation, or distress, or persecution, or famine, or nakedness, or danger, or sword shall not prevail over His love.

Do you trust His grasp, my children? Do you hope in the triumph of God alone, even when you are killed all the day long and regarded as sheep to be slaughtered? For in all these things we are more than conquerors through Him who loved us. You can be sure that neither death nor life, nor angels nor rulers, nor things present nor things to come, nor powers, nor height nor depth, nor anything else in all creation, will be able to separate us from the love of God in Christ Jesus our Lord (Romans 8).

*I have been driven many times to my knees by the overwhelming conviction that I had absolutely no other place to go.*
*~ Abraham Lincoln*

ffectual Lover,

Your purpose of election must stand, for it is beautiful and wise to choose a people not because of works but because of Your call. May my dear children learn to rejoice and tremble at Your words, "Jacob I loved, but Esau I hated." Let them not charge You with injustice because You are free. For You say to Moses, "I will have mercy on whom I have mercy, and I will have compassion on whom I have compassion." So then make them exult that it depends not on human will or exertion, but on You, who have mercy.

Let them love and fear the truth that You have mercy on whomever You will, and You harden whomever You will. Keep them from being men and women who question You with arrogance, or set their ways of justice above You, or demand You to account for what they find inequitable. May they not question their molder, saying, "Why have You made me like this?" For You are the Lord and potter, and to You belongs the right to make one vessel for honored use and another for dishonorable use.

My children, come, let us adore His goodness! In order to make known to us the riches of His glory He endured with much patience vessels of wrath prepared for destruction, to show His wrath and to make known His power.

Father, may Your Son be their greatest good forever. Amen (Romans 9).

reat Shepherd of Your sheep,
My heart's desire and prayer is that my children may be saved. Let them never be men and women who have a zeal for God, but not according to knowledge. Keep them from being ignorant of the righteousness that comes from You, and seeking to establish their own, thus failing to submit to Your righteousness. For Your Son is the end of the law for righteousness to everyone who believes.

Let this assurance ring afresh in their hearts: that if they confess with their mouths that Jesus is Lord and believe in their hearts that You raised Him from the dead, they will be saved.

My children, adore the free goodness of our Lord's salvation! For the Scripture says, "Everyone who believes in Him will not be put to shame." For there is no distinction between Jew and Greek; the same Lord is Lord of all, bestowing His riches on all who call on Him. For "everyone who calls on the name of the Lord will be saved."

Father, You have told us that faith comes through hearing, and hearing through the word of Christ. Therefore use my children to proclaim the good news so that their feet might be called beautiful. Amen (Romans 10).

*When thou prayest, rather let thy heart be without words, than thy words without a heart.* ~John Bunyan

agnificent God,

I appeal to You by Your mercies, to receive my lovely children's bodies as living sacrifices, holy and acceptable to You. And grant them the willingness to present their bodies in this way, as their spiritual worship. Let them not be conformed to this world, but transform them by the renewal of their minds, that by testing they may discern what Your will is, what is good and acceptable and perfect.

May they not think of themselves more highly than they ought to think, but rather think with sober judgment, according to the measure of faith that You have assigned. Enable them to use their gifts according to the grace given them: if prophecy, in proportion to their faith; if service, in their serving; if they teach, in their teaching; if they exhort, in their exhortation; if they contribute, in generosity; if they lead, with zeal; if they do acts of mercy, with cheerfulness.

My children, let your love be genuine. Abhor what is evil; hold fast to what is good. Love with brotherly affection. Let us outdo one another in showing honor. Do not be slothful in zeal, be fervent in spirit, serve the Lord.

Lord God, only by Your sovereign grace will they be able to rejoice in hope, be patient in tribulation, and be constant in prayer. Assist us together as we strive to contribute to the needs of the saints and seek to show hospitality. Amen (Romans 12).

wesome Lord,

Only by Your unmerited favor will my children grow in the likeness of Christ Jesus. So I entreat Your mercy on their behalf to enable them to bless those who persecute them; to bless and not curse them. Let them rejoice with those who rejoice, weep with those who weep, and live in harmony with their heavenly family. May they not be haughty, but associate with the lowly, giving themselves to humble tasks. Let them never be conceited, nor repay anyone evil for evil. Instead grant that they give thought to do what is honorable in the sight of all. If possible, so far as it depends on them, make them live peaceably with all.

My children, never avenge yourselves, but leave it to the wrath of God, for it is written, "Vengeance is mine, I will repay, says the LORD." To the contrary, if your enemy is hungry, feed him; if he is thirsty, give him something to drink; for by so doing you will heap burning coals on his head.

Holy God, do not let them be overcome by evil, but assist them to overcome evil with good; to cast off the works of darkness and put on the armor of light. Let them walk properly as in the daytime, not in orgies and drunkenness, not in sexual immorality and sensuality, not in quarreling and jealousy. But cause them to put on the Lord Jesus Christ, and make no provision for the flesh, to gratify its desires.

Come, Lord Jesus. We yearn for the day of Your unveiled beauty. Amen (Romans 12 & 13).

Thou who art faithful when we are faithless, Let my dear children not live to themselves. If they live, may they live to You, and if they die, may they die to You. So that whether they live or whether they die, they might be Yours. For to this end Christ died and lived again, that He might be Lord both of the dead and of the living.

My children, do not pass judgment on your sister, or despise your brother. For we will all stand before the judgment seat of God; for it is written, "As I live, says the Lord, every knee shall bow to me, and every tongue shall confess to God." So then we will both give an account of ourselves to God.

Therefore Father, let them not pass judgment on their brothers and sisters any longer, but rather decide never to put a stumbling block or hindrance in their way. Cause them to pursue what makes for peace and for mutual upbuilding.

Remind them of their obligation as men and women of strength to bear with the failings of the weak, and not to please themselves.

I ask, for the sake of Your Name, that through endurance and through the encouragement of the Scriptures they might have hope. May You enable us to live in such harmony with others, in accord with Christ Jesus, that together we may with one voice glorify You, the God and Father of our Lord Jesus Christ (Romans 14 & 15).

od of Hope,
May You fill my lovely children with all joy and peace in believing, so that by the power of the Holy Spirit they may abound in hope. Fill them also with goodness and with all knowledge, enabling them to instruct others.

I appeal to You, Lord God, to give my children discernment and vigilance to watch out for those who cause divisions and create obstacles contrary to the doctrine that they have been taught; may they avoid them. Safeguard them from their smooth talk and flattery by which they deceive the hearts of the naïve. For their obedience is known to all, so that I rejoice over them, but I want them to be wise as to what is good and innocent as to what is evil. Now to You who are able to strengthen them according to the gospel and the preaching of Jesus Christ, according to Your command, to bring about the obedience of faith—to You, the only wise God, be glory forevermore through Jesus Christ! Amen (Romans 15 & 16).

*Pray, and let God worry.* ~Martin Luther

hrist Jesus,

I praise You that in these last days God has spoken to us by You, His Son, whom He appointed heir of all things, through whom also He created the world.

Father, may my precious children take pleasure in beholding Your Son as the radiance of Your glory and the exact imprint of Your nature, as He upholds the universe by the word of His power. May they exalt Him as much superior to angels as the name He has inherited is more excellent than theirs.

My children, join with me in saying, "Your throne, Lord Christ, is forever and ever, the scepter of uprightness is the scepter of Your kingdom. You have loved righteousness and hated wickedness; therefore God, Your God, has anointed You with the oil of gladness beyond Your companions."

You, Lord, laid the foundation of the earth in the beginning, and the heavens are the work of Your hands; they will perish, but You remain; they will all wear out like a garment, like a robe You will roll them up, like a garment they will be changed. But You are the same, and Your years have no end.

Father, cause them to adore Your magnificent Son incessantly and abound in thanksgiving for every glimpse of His beauty.

We long to see Him face to face. Amen (Hebrews 1).

racious Father,

May my children consider Jesus, the apostle and high priest of our confession, who was faithful to You who appointed Him, just as Moses also was faithful in all Your house. For Jesus has been counted worthy of more glory than Moses—as much more glory as the builder of a house has more honor than the house itself. Now Moses was faithful in all Your house as a servant to testify to the things that were to be spoken later, but Christ is faithful over Your house as a son.

My children, we are His house if indeed we hold fast our confidence and our boasting in our hope.

Therefore Father, today, if they hear Your voice, let them not harden their hearts as in the rebellion. Take care of them, lest there be in them evil, unbelieving hearts, leading them to fall away from the living God.

Help us to exhort one another every day, as long as it is called "today," that neither of us may be hardened by the deceitfulness of sin. For we share in Christ, if indeed we hold our original confidence firm to the end. Enable us to endure steadfastly! Enable us so that we might gain Your glorious Son!

Amen, come quickly Lord Jesus (Hebrews 3).

*Prayer and means must go together. Means without prayer—presumption! Prayer without means—hypocrisy!*
~C.H. Spurgeon

od of the living word,

Only through Christ, the great high priest, who is better than angels and greater than Moses—only through Him do I intercede for my children. So I pray that while the promise of entering Your rest still stands they would fear lest they should seem to have failed to reach it. May Your good news meet with faith in them as they hear it.

I praise You that there remains a Sabbath rest for Your people, for whoever has entered Your rest has also rested from their works as You did from Yours. As the Scriptures say, "And God rested on the seventh day from all His works."

Let my cherished children therefore strive to enter that rest, so that they may not fall by the same sort of disobedience that overtook all those who left Egypt led by Moses. For Your word is living and active, sharper than any two-edged sword, piercing to the division of soul and of spirit, of joints and of marrow, and discerning the thoughts and intentions of the heart. And no creature is hidden from Your sight, but all are naked and exposed to Your eyes. And to You we must give an account.

My children, since we have a great high priest who has passed through the heavens, Jesus, the Son of God, let us hold fast our confession. For we do not have a high priest who is unable to sympathize with our weaknesses, but one who in every respect has been tempted as we are, yet without sin. Let us then with confidence draw near to the throne of grace, that we may receive mercy and find grace in our time of need (Hebrews 4).

plendid Savior,
It is my joy to trust and exalt You as the perfect source of eternal salvation to all who obey You.

Father, through Your Son I ask that my wonderful children would never become dull of hearing, but instead crave solid food, developing skill in the word of righteousness. For solid food is for the mature. Therefore, please train their powers of discernment by constant practice to distinguish good from evil.

My children, let us leave the elementary doctrine of Christ and go on to maturity, not laying again a foundation of repentance from dead works and of faith toward God. And this we will do if God permits.

Therefore, Father, please be willing! Please permit them to go on to maturity. Keep them, and may they never be as those who are enlightened, taste the heavenly gift, share in the Holy Spirit, taste of the goodness of Your word, and then fall away. May it never be! (Hebrews 5 & 6).

*I must secure more time for private devotions. I have been living far too public for me. The shortening of devotions starves the soul, it grows lean and faint. I have been keeping too late hours.* ~William Wilberforce

od of boundless mercy,

May my dear children live as land that has drunk the rain that often falls on it, and produces a crop useful to those for whose sake it is cultivated, so that they might receive a blessing from You. But have mercy on them lest they bear thorns and thistles, for such land is worthless and near to being cursed, and its end is to be burned.

Assure them of better things—things that belong to salvation. And I desire Your work in them, causing them to show the same earnestness to have the full assurance of hope until the end, so that they may not be sluggish, but imitators of those who through faith and patience inherit the promises.

Remind them of the unchangeable character of Your purpose, that they might have strong encouragement to hold fast to the hope set before them.

My children, flee for refuge to Christ! For God has sworn by Himself and we have this promise as a sure and steadfast anchor of the soul, a hope that enters into the inner place behind the curtain, where Jesus has gone as a forerunner on our behalf, having become a high priest forever after the order of Melchizedek.

Lord Jesus, we exalt You as our hope and high priest! Please do not tarry in Your return (Hebrews 6).

lofty Lover of broken men,
I come to You on behalf of my children through Jesus, the guarantor of a better covenant. Instill within them the wondrous assurance that Christ holds His priesthood permanently, because He continues forever. Consequently, He is able to save to the uttermost those who draw near to You through Him, since He always lives to make intercession for them. May they entrust themselves wholly to Him, for it is fitting that they should have such a high priest, holy, innocent, unstained, separated from sinners, and exalted above the heavens.

May they exalt Him, for He has no need, like other high priests, to offer sacrifices daily, first for His own sins and then for those of the people, since He did this once for all when he offered up Himself. For the law appoints men in their weakness as high priests, but the word of the oath, which came later than the law, appoints a Son who has been made perfect forever. Let them cling to Him all the more!

Father, assist us to love the Son's appearing (Hebrews 7).

*There is not in the world a kind of life more sweet and delightful than that of a continual conversation with God.* ~Brother Lawrence

God, my wealth and my salvation, Sink deep within my priceless children the understanding that they have a perfect and powerful high priest, one who is seated at the right hand of the throne of the Majesty in heaven, a minister in the holy places in the true tent that You set up, not man. For Christ has obtained a ministry that is as much more excellent than the old as the covenant He mediates is better, since it is enacted on better promises. Cause them to trust Christ's sacrifice alone, who through the eternal Spirit offered Himself without blemish to You. By His blood purify their conscience from dead works to serve You.

Take heart, my children, for Christ, having been offered once to bear the sins of many, will appear a second time, not to deal with sin but to save those who are eagerly waiting for Him.

Father, grant them such eagerness, that they may look forward to the day when their glorified Savior returns. May they exult in His sacrifice, offered once for all time for sins, after which He sat down at Your right hand, waiting for that time until His enemies should be made a footstool for His feet. O let them praise and prize Him! For by a single offering He has perfected for all time those who are being sanctified (Hebrews 8, 9, 10).

*Prayer is as much a tool of our sanctification, by God's grace, as it is a tool of ministering God's grace to others.* ~Bruce Ware

earful Judge,

Since my adorable children now have confidence to enter the holy places by the blood of Jesus, by the new and living way that He opened for them through the curtain, that is, through His flesh, and since they have a great high priest over Your house, let them draw near to You with a true heart in full assurance of faith, with their hearts sprinkled clean from an evil conscience and their bodies washed with pure water. May they hold fast the confession of their hope without wavering, for You who promised are faithful.

My children, let us consider how to stir one another to love and good works, not neglecting our time together, as is the habit of some, but encouraging one another, and all the more as we see the Day drawing near.

Father, keep them from going on sinning deliberately after receiving the knowledge of the truth, for if they do there no longer remains a sacrifice for sins, but a fearful expectation of judgment, and a fury of fire that will consume the adversaries. Please, please prevent them from spurning Your Son, or profaning the blood of the covenant by which they were sanctified, or outraging the Spirit of grace! For I know that vengeance is Yours; You will repay. "The Lord will judge His people." Sustain them! For it is a fearful thing to fall into the hands of the living God (Hebrews 10).

elf-sufficient God,

Only by Your worthy Son do I come to petition transforming and supporting grace for my children. Because in You are all good things infinitely, I ask that they would grow in kindness and sympathy. Make them men and women who have compassion on those in prison, and who joyfully accept the plundering of their property, knowing that they have a better possession and an abiding one. Let them not throw away their confidence, which has a great reward. For they have need of endurance, so that when they have done Your will they may receive what is promised. May they not be of those who shrink back and are destroyed, but of those who have faith and preserve their souls.

Raise them up as men and women of faith, having the assurance of things hoped for, the conviction of things not seen. For without faith it is impossible to please You, for whoever would draw near to You must believe that You exist and that You reward those who seek You.

My children, even though men and women of old were commended through their faith, they did not receive what was promised, since God had provided something better for us, that apart from us they should not be made perfect. And now we have the Lord Jesus Christ! Bless His name with me!

Father, we long to see Your matchless Son. Let us praise His name forever, to Your glory. Amen (Hebrews 10 & 11).

isciplining Father,

Assist my children to lay aside every weight, and sin which clings so closely, and let them run with endurance the race that is set before them, looking to Jesus, the founder and perfecter of their faith, who for the joy that was set before Him endured the cross, despising the shame, and is seated at the right hand of Your throne.

My children, consider Him who endured from sinners such hostility against Himself, so that you may not grow weary or fainthearted. In our struggle against sin we have not yet resisted to the point of shedding our blood.

Great Father, remind them of the exhortation that addresses them as sons: "My son, do not regard lightly the discipline of the Lord, nor be weary when reproved by Him. For the Lord disciplines the one He loves, and chastises every son whom He receives."

Assure them that it is for discipline that they have to endure—that You are treating them as sons and daughters. For if they are left without discipline, in which all have participated, then they are illegitimate children and not sons. May they not begrudge Your correction, but respect You and be subject to You, understanding that You discipline them for their good, that they may share in Your holiness. When Your discipline seems painful rather than pleasant, make them confident that later it yields the peaceful fruit of righteousness to those who have been trained by it (Hebrews 12).

entle and fearful Healer,

I bow through the merit of my Lord Christ, asking that You would lift my children's drooping hands and strengthen their weak knees, and make straight paths for their feet, so that what is lame may not be put out of joint but rather be healed.

Cause them to strive for peace with everyone, and for the holiness without which no one will see You. May it never be that they fail to obtain Your grace! Protect them from any "root of bitterness" that springs up, causes trouble, and defiles many. Look after and guard their ways, that they may not be sexually immoral or unholy like Esau, who sold his birthright for a single meal. Have mercy! For I know that afterward, when he desired to inherit the blessing, he was rejected, for he found no chance to repent, though he sought it with tears.

My children, take refuge in Jesus, the mediator of a new covenant. See that you do not refuse the warnings of His Father. Flee to Christ, and you need not fear.

Father, help us as we strive to offer to You acceptable worship, with reverence and awe. For You are a consuming fire. Amen (Hebrews 12).

*Satan trembles when he sees*
*The weakest saint upon his knees.*
~William Cowper

aithful Helper,

Under the supreme sacrifice of Your Son I come on behalf of my beautiful children. Please form them into men and women who do not neglect to show hospitality to strangers, for thereby some have entertained angels unawares. May they remember those who are in prison, as though in prison with them, and those who are mistreated.

Raise them up to hold marriage in honor, and keep their marriage beds undefiled, for You will judge the sexually immoral and adulterous. Maintain their lives free from the love of money, and make them content with what they have, for You have said, "I will never leave you nor forsake you."

Therefore, my children, you can confidently say, "The Lord is my helper; I will not fear; what can man do to me?"

Father, remind them of their leaders, those who spoke to them Your word. May they consider the outcome of their way of life, and imitate their faith, for Jesus Christ is the same yesterday and today and forever. Guard them from being led away by diverse and strange teachings, for it is good for the heart to be strengthened by grace, not by the food of carnal wisdom, which has not benefited those devoted to it.

Hasten the day of Your Son's appearing, we pray. Amen (Hebrews 13).

y dazzling Delight,

Through Christ Jesus I ask that You would put a willingness in my children's hearts to bear the reproach Your Son endured. May they grow to love the world less and love You more; to love me less and love You more. For here we have no lasting city, but we seek the city that is to come. Through Christ then let them continually offer up a sacrifice of praise to You, that is, the fruit of lips that acknowledge His name. Let them not neglect to do good and to share what they have, for such sacrifices are pleasing to You.

Help them to obey us as leaders and submit to us, for we are keeping watch over their souls, as those who will have to give an account.

O my children, adore with me the God that gives you worth! May the God of peace who brought again from the dead our Lord Jesus, the great shepherd of the sheep, by the blood of the eternal covenant, equip you with everything good that you may do His will, working in you that which is pleasing in His sight, through Jesus Christ, to whom be glory forever and ever. Amen (Hebrews 13).

y Sovereign Joy,

By Your beautiful Son and in His words I pray for my delightful children. May they be counted among the poor in spirit, for theirs is the kingdom of heaven. Make them of those who mourn, for they shall be comforted. Bless them with meekness so that they will inherit the earth. Create within them a hunger and thirst for righteousness, for such shall be satisfied. Let them be merciful so that they may receive mercy. Give them pure hearts so that they might see You. Number them among the peacemakers, for they shall be called Your children. When they are persecuted for righteousness' sake, may they be heartened that they are blessed and that theirs is the kingdom of heaven.

My children, let me remind you that you are blessed when others revile you and persecute you and utter all kinds of evil against you falsely on Christ's account. Rejoice and be glad, for your reward is great in heaven, for so they persecuted the prophets who were before you.

LORD, please be ever at work in them, molding them to be like Your Son. Amen (Matthew 5).

y gracious Father,

Through Jesus I kneel and ask that You would make my priceless children a brilliant light to the world. Let their light shine before others, so that they may see their good works and glorify You.

May they do Your commandments and teach them so that they will be called great in the kingdom of heaven. For unless their righteousness exceeds that of the scribes and Pharisees, they will never enter the kingdom of heaven. Keep them from becoming angry with their neighbor, from murdering him in their hearts, and thus becoming liable to judgment. Keep them from looking at others with lustful intent, from committing adultery in their hearts. If their right eyes cause them to sin, let them tear them out and throw them away. For I would rather them lose one of their members than have their whole bodies thrown into hell. Instill within them a healthy fear of eternal fire.

Grant them humble longsuffering so as not to resist the person who is evil. If anyone slaps them on the right cheek, let them turn to him the other also. And if anyone would sue them and take their tunics, may they let him have their cloaks as well. And if anyone forces them to go one mile, let them go with him two miles. Make them men and women who give to the one who begs from them, and who do not refuse the one who would borrow from them (Matthew 5).

oving Shepherd,

Please listen to my prayer because of Your Son's righteousness. I ask that You would incline the hearts of my sweet children to obey His commands. May they love their enemies and pray for those who persecute them, so that they may be Your children. For You make Your sun rise on the evil and the good, and send rain on the just and on the unjust.

My children, if you love those who love you, what reward do you have? Does not even the world do the same? You therefore must be perfect, as your heavenly Father is perfect.

Lord, by Your Spirit continually work Your perfection in them! Help them to abstain from practicing their righteousness before other people in order to be seen by them, for then they will have no reward from You.

When they give to the needy, do not let their left hands know what their right hands are doing, so that their giving may be in secret. For then You who see in secret will reward them.

And when they pray, keep them from being like the hypocrites who love to be seen and heard by others. Instead, cause them to go into their rooms and shut the door and pray to You who see in secret. Then, for what You see in secret please reward them. Amen (Matthew 5 & 6).

aithful Father,

Through Your Son I ask that You would keep my children obeying His words. May they not lay up for themselves treasures on earth, where moth and rust destroy and where thieves break in and steal, but make them lay up for themselves treasures in heaven, where neither moth nor rust destroys and where thieves do not break in and steal. For where their treasure is, there their hearts will be also. And I long for their hearts to love You unswervingly as their Treasure. They cannot serve two masters; they cannot serve You and money. Therefore keep them always as Your joyful, loyal servants.

Let them not be anxious about their lives, what they will eat or what they will drink, nor about their bodies, what they will put on. For life is more than food, and the body more than clothing. Turn their eyes to the birds of the air and remind them—they neither sow nor reap nor gather into barns, and yet You feed them. And they are of much more value than the birds! Remind them that they cannot add a single hour to their span of life by being anxious. Guard them from being anxious about clothing, for the lilies of the field neither toil nor spin, yet even Solomon in all his glory was not arrayed like one of them.

My children, trust your Master, lest He say, "O you of little faith." For if He clothes the grass of the field, which today is alive and tomorrow is thrown into the oven, will He not much more clothe you? Therefore do not be anxious, saying, "What shall we eat?" or "What shall we drink?" or "What shall we wear?" For everyone seeks after all these things, and your heavenly Father knows that you need them all. But seek first the kingdom of God and His righteousness, and all these things will be added to you.

Therefore, Father, may they not be anxious about tomorrow, for tomorrow will be anxious for itself. Sufficient for the day is its own trouble (Matthew 6).

*I would exhort those who have entertained a hope of their being true converts—and who since their supposed conversion have left off the duty of secret prayer, and ordinarily allow themselves in the omission of it—to throw away their hope. If you have left off calling upon God, it is time for you to leave off hoping and flattering yourselves with an imagination that you are the children of God. Probably it will be a very difficult thing for you to do this. It is hard for a man to let go a hope of heaven, on which he hath once allowed himself to lay hold, and which he hath retained for a considerable time. True conversion is a rare thing; but that men should be brought off from a false hope of conversion—after they are once settled and established in it, and have continued in it for some time—is much more rare.*
~Jonathan Edwards

verlasting King,

I bow through Christ for the sake of the children You have granted me. May they judge not, that they be not judged. For with the judgment they pronounce they will be judged, and with the measure they use it will be measured to them. Guide them away from hypocrisy, to first take the log out of their own eyes, so that then they will see clearly to take the speck out of their brother's eye.

Make them wise to avoid giving dogs what is holy, and to not throw their pearls before pigs, lest they trample them underfoot and turn to attack them.

Cause them to ask, so that it will be given to them; to seek, so that they will find; to knock, so that it will be opened to them. Thank You for Your promise that everyone who asks receives, and the one who seeks finds, and to the one who knocks it will be opened. Remind them that if I, who am evil, know how to give good gifts to my children, how much more will their Father who is in heaven give good things to those who ask Him!

Whatever they wish that others would do to them, help them do also to them, for this is the Law and the Prophets. May they enter by the narrow gate. For the gate is wide and the way is easy that leads to destruction, and those who enter by it are many. For the gate is narrow and the way is hard that leads to life, and those who find it are few. Keep them steadfast on the hard way! May they never stray from it! For Your namesake let their feet not slip. Amen (Matthew 7).

ighteous Father,
Please protect my children from false prophets, who come in sheep's clothing but inwardly are ravenous wolves. Make them wise to recognize them by their fruits. Help them to discern the healthy tree by its good fruit, and the diseased tree by its bad fruit. May they not be diseased trees, for every such tree is cut down and thrown into the fire. Therefore, help them to bear much good fruit.

Let the warning of Your Son safeguard and preserve them when He says, "Not everyone who says to me, 'Lord, Lord,' will enter the kingdom of heaven, but the one who does the will of my Father who is in heaven." May He not say to them, "I never knew you; depart from me, you workers of lawlessness." No! Instead, please let them hear the words, "Well done, good and faithful servant." Through Jesus and by Your wonderful Spirit I ask these things (Matthew 7 & 25).

*The Spirit has much to do with acceptable prayer, and His work in prayer is too much neglected. He enlightens the mind to see its wants, softens the heart to feel them, quickens our desires after suitable supplies, gives clear views of God's power, wisdom, and grace to relieve us, and stirs up that confidence in His truth which excludes all wavering. Prayer is, therefore, a wonderful thing. In every acceptable prayer the whole Trinity is concerned. ~J. Angell James*

evealer of Truth,

Through Christ I ask that You would make my darling children hear His words and do them, so that they may be like a wise man who built his house on a rock. Keep them from merely hearing His words and not doing them, for then they will be like the foolish man who built his house on the sand. When the rain falls, and the floods come, and the winds blow and beat against them, I do not wish them to fall! Your Word alone stands firm. May they build their lives upon it.

Let them never despise or neglect tax collectors and sinners. But instead fill them with tenderness and compassion for them, and the humility to eat with them. For those who are well have no need of a physician, but those who are sick. Continue to teach them what this means: "I desire mercy, and not sacrifice." For Your great Son came not to call the righteous, but sinners (Matthew 7 & 9).

y Supreme and Everlasting Joy,

In this world my children are as sheep in the midst of wolves, so please help them to be wise as serpents and innocent as doves. Prepare them for the persecution that lies along their pathway to heaven. Strengthen them to stand fast when men deliver them over to courts and flog them in their churches.

My children, when you are dragged before governors and kings for Christ's sake, do not be anxious how you are to speak or what you are to say, for what you are to say will be given to you in that hour. For it is not you who speak, but the Spirit of your Father speaking through you.

Lord God, make ready their hearts for that dreadful time when brother will deliver brother over to death, and the father his child, and children will rise up against parents and have them put to death, and they will be hated by all for the sake of Christ's name. May they endure to the end and so be saved! Keep them! For Your hand is mightier than my own. Amen (Matthew 10).

❧

*Prayer—secret, fervent, believing prayer—lies at the root of all*
*personal godliness.* ~William Carey

electable God,

Grant my dear children the grace to love Christ more than their father or mother, more than their son or daughter. For Your Son has said that if they fail to love Him supremely, they are not worthy of Him. And if they do not take their cross and follow Him, they are not worthy of Him. Therefore, because of Your grace and steadfast love, enable them to do so!

May they not find their lives in this world and so lose them, but make them men and women who gladly lose their lives for Jesus' sake so that they might find them.

Father, I know that it pleases You well to hide things from the wise and understanding and reveal them to little children. Therefore please grow them in childlikeness, show them Your matchless Son, and may He choose to reveal You increasingly to them.

My children, you who labor and are heavy laden, go to Christ, and He will give you rest. Take His yoke upon you, and learn from Him, for He is gentle and lowly in heart, and you will find rest for your souls.

Lord Christ, we praise and thank You that Your yoke is easy, and Your burden is light! (Matthew 10 & 11).

reat Covenant Keeper,

My children cannot speak good if they are evil. For out of the abundance of the heart the mouth speaks. Therefore fill them with good treasure so that they might bring forth good. Make Christ their Treasure, so that they might speak His praise. For on the day of judgment they will give account for every careless word they speak; so please do not let them be condemned by their words.

Let them never be among those of whom it is said, "Seeing they do not see, and hearing they do not hear, nor do they understand." Keep their hearts from growing dull. Help them to see with their eyes and hear with their ears and understand with their hearts and turn, that You may heal them.

Father, it is You who must open their eyes to behold the wonders of Your word and the glories of Your Son. Keep them vigilant. Amen (Matthew 12 & 13).

*No man can do me a truer kindness in this world*
*than to pray for me.* ~Charles Spurgeon

elf-exalting God,

May my precious children never prove themselves to be as those who, when they hear the word of the kingdom and do not understand it, the evil one comes and snatches away what has been sown in their hearts. Guard them from the evil one! And let them not be like those who hear the word and immediately receive it with joy, yet they have no root in themselves, but endure for a while, and when tribulation or persecution arises on account of the word, immediately they fall away. Do not let them fall! Please grow their roots strong and deep in You.

Save them from being men and women who hear the word, but the cares of the world and the deceitfulness of riches choke the word, and it proves unfruitful. Instead, make their hearts good soil, so that they hear the word and understand it, and bear fruit and yield a hundredfold (Matthew 13).

overeign Ruler and King,
Your Kingdom is like treasure hidden in a field,
which a man found and covered up. Therefore,
may my children be like that man, who, in his joy went and
sold all that he had and bought the field.

Again, make them like the merchant in search of fine
pearls, who, on finding one pearl of great value, went and
sold all that he had and bought it. Let them count Christ their
greatest treasure, their most valuable pearl, their ultimate
source of joy. And may they stop at nothing to have Him.

Keep them from breaking Your commandments for the
sake of tradition. May they never, for the sake of tradition,
make void Your word. Indeed, unless You preserve them with
grace they will be numbered among the hypocrites who honor
You with their lips, but their hearts are far from You; who
worship You in vain, teaching as doctrines the commandments of men.

Let them take heart, and not be afraid, for it is You who
keep them. Let them not doubt, for truly Jesus, the Son of
God, is their righteousness (Matthew 13, 14, 15).

*No praying man or woman accomplishes so much with so little
expenditure of time as when he or she is praying.*
~A.E. McAdam

ord of the heavens and the earth,

I come to You now petitioning more grace for my children. Their hearts need continual cleansing, as does mine, because what proceeds from it is what defiles a person. For out of the heart come evil thoughts, murder, adultery, sexual immorality, theft, false witness, slander. These are what defile a person, therefore please create in them clean hearts.

My children, guard your hearts. Watch and beware of the leaven of the Pharisees and Sadducees, of the sophistry of this age, of the false teachers who speak sweetly and humbly. Blessed are you if you know the truth of Christ. For flesh and blood has not revealed Him to you, but your Father who is in heaven.

O God, may they set their minds on the things of You, and not on the things of man. All this I ask in the name of the Christ, the Son of the living God. Amen (Matthew 15 & 16).

*All hell is vanquished when the believer bows his knee in importunate supplication. Beloved brethren, let us pray. We cannot all argue, but we can all pray; we cannot all be leaders, but we can all be pleaders; we cannot all be mighty in rhetoric, but we can all be prevalent in prayer. I would sooner see you eloquent with God than with men. Prayer links us with the Eternal, the Omnipotent, the Infinite, and hence it is our chief resort. . . . Be sure that you are with God, and then you may be sure that God is with you.* ~Charles Spurgeon

*Every once and a while in the midst of this darkness, a dim light would flash and I'd hear the words, "This is a spiritual battle. Pray for her." But prayer is the last thing anyone wants to do in crisis. Sure, you pray, but it's not where your main energy goes. Your main energy goes into worrying, fearing, plotting, strategizing. Your imagination paints lurid scenarios and your brain works overtime, spewing out plan after plan to stave off encroaching doom.*
*How hard this is! We don't mind praying so long as we can keep on worrying too. We Christian parents would not be caught bowing down before a pagan shrine, but night after night we kneel and worry beside our children's beds. We think we are praying, but we are not. We are worrying, and there is nothing godly, virtuous, or even practical about worry.* ~Mike Mason

oly Lord,

Compared to the rest of the world my children are astonishingly rich. And only with difficulty will a rich person enter the kingdom of heaven. Therefore, if they will be saved, You must do what is impossible with man—give them hearts that cherish You more than money, possessions, or comfort. Help them! For it is easier for a camel to go through the eye of a needle than for a rich person to enter Your kingdom. Praise be to Your name that with You all things are possible—that they and I can be saved!

Grant them the grace to leave houses or brothers or sisters or father or mother or children or lands, for the sake of Christ's name, so that they might receive a hundredfold and inherit eternal life. Amen (Matthew 19).

ighteous Father,

There are so many pitfalls of hypocrisy that threaten to destroy my children. You alone can guard their footsteps from straying from the narrow path. Let them never become as those who do all their deeds to be seen by others, loving the place of honor at feasts and the admiration of churches and greetings in the marketplaces and being called wise by others.

My children, do not glory in your wisdom, for all you have is because of Jesus. For you have an instructor, the Christ. Whoever exalts himself will be humbled, and whoever humbles himself will be exalted.

Again, Father, may they never shut the kingdom of heaven in people's faces. Spare them from becoming children of hell! Have mercy and save them from such woe (Matthew 23).

*I have so much business I cannot get on without spending three hours daily in prayer.* ~Martin Luther

Thou who art beauty's fairest pleasure, Protect my children. They dwell in a deceitful world; guard their minds. Keep them safe from blind guides and blind fools. Save them from following those who tithe generously and have neglected the weightier matters of the law: justice and mercy and faithfulness. May they not neglect these things, lest they be like the blind guides who strain out a gnat and swallow a camel!

Shield them also from the snare of merely external righteousness, like those who clean the outside of the cup and plate, but inside they are full of greed and self-indulgence. Please make them clean inside, that their outside also may be clean. Again, preserve them from becoming like whitewashed tombs, which outwardly appear beautiful, but within are full of dead people's bones and all uncleanness. Woe to them if You do not rescue them from being children who outwardly appear righteous to others, but within are full of hypocrisy and lawlessness (Matthew 23).

*Prayer is designed by God to display his fullness and our need.*
*Prayer glorifies God because it puts us in the position of the*
*thirsty and God in the position of the all-supplying fountain.*
~John Piper

ighty Ruler,

Please, because of Christ, hear my prayer, and see that no one leads my precious children astray. For many will come in Jesus' name, saying, "I am the Christ," and they will lead many astray. And when they hear of wars and rumors of wars, see that they are not alarmed.

My children, do not be surprised or afraid when kingdoms deliver us up to tribulation and put us to death. For the Son has warned us that we will be hated by all nations for His name's sake.

O Father, when many then fall away and betray one another and hate one another, let them not be found among them! Protect them from the many false prophets that will arise and lead many astray. And when lawlessness increases, do not let their love grow cold. But help them to endure to the end and be saved, and proclaim the gospel of the kingdom throughout the whole world as a testimony to all nations. Amen (Matthew 24).

Lover of the sheep,
Only You can keep my children for Jesus Christ when He comes in His glory and sits on His glorious throne. So I ask that You would preserve them as Your sheep, to whom the Son of Man will say on that day, "Come, you who are blessed by my Father, inherit the kingdom prepared for you from the foundation of the world."

May they be men and women who feed the hungry, give drink to the thirsty, welcome the stranger, clothe the naked, and visit the sick and imprisoned.

My children, truly, I say to you, as you do it to one of the least of these, you do it to Christ.

Father, it is my fervent desire that they be such righteous men and women so that they might enter into eternal life. Thank You for the promise that, as they strive to enter by the narrow gate, Christ is with them always, to the end of the age.

Our great Savior and King, we long for Your return. Amen (Matthew 25 & 28).

*You cannot simply manipulate God by the power of being confident in what you ask. There are moral guidelines. This is what Jesus is saying with the condition, "If . . . my words abide in you, ask whatever you wish, and it will be done for you" (John 15:7). The words of Jesus shape the attitude and content of our prayers.* ~John Piper

ord and Husband,

When my beloved children stray from Your love, however wicked their waywardness proves to be, please draw them back! Even when they forget You, allure them, and bring them into the wilderness, and speak tenderly to them. Make the Valley of Trouble a door of hope for them. May they answer You as in the days of their youth, as at the time when they came out of the land of bondage. And let them call You "My Husband." Make them lie down in safety and remind them that You have betrothed them to Yourself forever.

My children, forsake not your Husband! For He has betrothed you to Himself in righteousness and in justice, in steadfast love and in mercy. He has betrothed you to Himself in faithfulness. And you have known Him!

Father, be pleased to guard them from abandoning faithfulness, steadfast love, and the knowledge of You. Save them from being destroyed for lack of knowledge, from forsaking You to cherish whoredom, wine, and new wine, which take away the understanding. Preserve us all, for a people without understanding shall come to ruin (Hosea 2 & 4).

*Praying is the same to the new creature as crying is to the natural. The child is not learned by art or example to cry, but instructed by nature; it comes into the world crying. Praying is not a lesson got by forms and rules of art, but flowing from principles of new life itself.*
~William Gurnall

ost Holy Judge,

My precious children are not immune to the subtle deceitfulness of sin. Therefore please protect them; increase their wisdom. Let them not be like doves, silly and without sense. Woe to them if they stray from You! Only destruction will they find if You do not keep them.

May they never cry falsely, "My God, I—Your child—know You," when they have transgressed Your covenant and rebelled against Your law. Restrain them from making idols with their silver and gold. And forbid that they ever become incapable of innocence.

My children, fear the LORD and turn away from evil, lest you find yourselves to be useless vessels, and begin to regard His laws as a strange thing.

Father, may they not forget their Maker! Let them not grow to love wages of unfaithfulness. May they consecrate themselves always to You and not to anything shameful, lest they become detestable like the thing they love. Preserve their glory and righteousness, and do not give my daughters miscarrying wombs and dry breasts. Accept them because they listen to You, and make them bear much fruit in Your house. Show Your love to them, that their children may see many days (Hosea 7, 8, 9).

*Many avoid prayer because they find no joy in it. They find no joy because they either ritualize the life out of prayer, turning it into something they cannot bear, or else squeeze it into such cramped spaces that it feels like a wolfed breakfast rather than a relaxed, candlelit dinner. Prayer is the language of love, of intimate relationship. Give up trying to please the boss.*
~Mike Mason

erciful Leader of wayward children,

Thank You for growing my children into luxuriant vines that yield their fruit. You have dealt bountifully in giving them to me. But as their fruit increases, may they not use it to improve their pursuit of self or foreign altars. Guard their hearts from becoming false, saying, "I have no king, for I do not fear the LORD." Such is the danger if You do not keep them. Unless You continue with them they will utter mere words; with empty oaths they will make covenants. Let them not be put to shame!

My children, He has kindly spared your necks. Do not make Him put you to the yoke to plow and harrow for yourself. Instead, sow for yourselves righteousness; reap steadfast love.

LORD God, break up their fallow ground and let them seek You, that You may come and rain righteousness upon them.

Have mercy on us, for we have together plowed iniquity; we have reaped injustice; we have eaten the fruit of lies. We have trusted in our own way; do not destroy us! Because of our great evil we appeal to the righteousness of Christ, for apart from Him we should be dashed in pieces and utterly cut off.

O great Son of David, we praise Your Name and bow with trembling, thankful hearts. Hasten Your glorious return! Amen (Hosea 10).

ost High Father,

Please teach my children to walk; take them up by their arms, and heal them. Let them rejoice and sing for joy as You lead them with cords of kindness, with the bands of love. And so become to them as one who eases the yoke on their jaws, and bend down to them and fed them.

My children, take care, and keep your souls diligently, lest you forget the things that your eyes have seen, and lest they depart from your heart all the days of your life.

Sovereign LORD, when their hearts are bent on turning away from You, may Your compassion grow warm and tender. On account of Christ Jesus do not execute Your burning anger; for You are God and not a man, the Holy One in our midst, and because of Your great mercy do not come in wrath.

If they stray, roar like a lion, so that when You roar they will come trembling—trembling like a bird from Egypt. Then may they walk with You and remain faithful to the Holy One (Hosea 11 & Deuteronomy 4).

*I had rather learn what some men really judge about their own justification from their* prayers *than their writings.* ~John Owen

ORD God of hosts,
May my children, by Your help, hold fast to love and justice, and wait continually for You. Keep them from incurring guilt and forsaking Christ. For if they do they shall be like the morning mist or like the dew that goes early away, like the chaff that swirls from the threshing floor or like smoke from a window. You are the LORD our God; we know no God but You, and besides You there is no savior. It was You who knew them in the wilderness, in the land of drought. But now, when they are filled, and their hearts are lifted up, let them not forget You.

Even when they turn away from their Helper, because of Christ, do not destroy them. I thank You for His sacrifice on their behalf, so that You will not devour them and rip them open in Your wrath.

My children, bless the Name of Jesus, for He can ransome you from the power of Sheol! He is able to redeem you from Death. O Death, where are your plagues? O Sheol, where is your sting? The sting of death is sin, and the power of sin is the law. But thanks be to God, who gives us the victory through our Lord Jesus Christ.

LORD God, let not compassion be hidden from Your eyes toward them. May they flourish, and may their fountain never dry up. Amen (Hosea 12, 13, I Corinthians 15).

ORD God of Israel,
Continue in faithful mercy toward my most treasured children. Turn Your anger from them and love them freely. Be like the dew to them, causing them to blossom like the lily, and take root like the trees of Lebanon. Then their shoots shall spread out; their beauty shall be like the olive, and their fragrance like Lebanon. Let them dwell beneath Your shadow; may they flourish like the grain and blossom like the vine; make their fame be like the wine of Lebanon.

My children, what has our LORD God to do with idols? It is He who answers and looks after you. He is like an evergreen cypress; from Him comes your fruit.

Sovereign LORD, let them be wise and understand these things; give them discernment to know them; for Your ways are right, and the upright walk in them, but transgressors stumble in them (Hosea 14).

*In God's commands to pray, we are compelled by the force of divine authority to come and drink of the living water, to receive bread from heaven, and to realize afresh moment by moment by moment that all that we long for, and everything that is good, is found in one and only one place: in God.*
~Bruce Ware

ORD of Zion,

Thank You that through Christ my lovely children are washed; they are made clean; the evil of their deeds is removed from before Your eyes because He has borne their punishment. Assist them now to cease to do evil, learn to do good, seek justice, correct oppression, bring justice to the fatherless, plead the widow's cause.

Come now, children, let us reason together: though your sins were like scarlet, they are now white as snow; though they were red like crimson, they have now become like wool. Trust Christ for your righteousness! He is a great Savior.

Come, LORD God, and lead them up to Your mountain, to the house of the God of Jacob, that You may teach them Your ways and that they may walk in Your paths. O LORD, let them walk in Your light.

Let them stop regarding man in whose nostrils is breath, for of what account is he? Instead, give them more regard for Christ, so that on the day of the LORD they will not need to hide in the dust from before Your terror, and from the splendor of Your majesty. Prepare us together for that day, when the haughty looks of man shall be brought low, and the lofty pride of men shall be humbled, and You alone will be exalted (Isaiah 1 & 2).

ternal Source of all good,

Please continue to restrain the wicked inclinations that remain in my children's hearts. For if You do not, they will soon become haughty and walk with out-stretched necks, glancing wantonly with their eyes. Go on with Your work of making them holy, washing away the filth of Your sons and daughters, and cleansing their bloodstains by a spirit of purging.

Thank You for loving them as a choice vineyard, and planting them with choice vines on a fertile hill. Now let them yield grapes, and not wild grapes.

My children, you are the LORD's pleasant planting. Therefore, do not feast with tambourine and flute and wine, and disregard the deeds of the LORD, or turn a blind eye to the work of His hands.

LORD of hosts, let them never be found lacking in the knowledge of You, so that they may not condemn themselves to exile, hunger, and thirst. For before You man is humbled, and each one is brought low, and the eyes of the haughty are brought low. But You are exalted in justice, and You show Yourself holy in righteousness (Isaiah 3, 4, 5).

*I have been benefited by praying for others; for by making an errand to God for them I have gotten something for myself.*
~Samuel Rutherford

ORD of hosts,

Guard my tender children from those who draw iniquity with cords of falsehood, who draw sin as with cart ropes. Protect them from those who call evil good and good evil, who put darkness for light and light for darkness, who put bitter for sweet and sweet for bitter! There are many who are wise in their own eyes, and shrewd in their own sight; let them not be found among them. Make them stand firm and humble in the midst of those who are heroes at drinking wine, who acquit the guilty for a bribe, and deprive the innocent of his right. For they have rejected Your law, and have despised the word of the Holy One of Israel. Therefore, their root will be as rottenness, and their blossom will go up like dust.

My children, sing with me the words of the seraphim. "Holy, holy, holy is the LORD of hosts; the whole earth is full of His glory!" Behold, through Christ your guilt is taken away, and your sin atoned for. Therefore, you can now rejoice when your eyes see the King, the LORD of hosts.

Help them to remain firm in faith, O LORD. For if they are not firm in faith, they will not be firm at all. And let them not fear what the world fears, nor be in dread. But You, O LORD of hosts—may they regard You as holy. May You be their fear, and may You be their dread. Amen (Isaiah 5, 6, 7, 8).

mniscient Father,

Thank You that my dearest children who walked in darkness have seen a great light; they used to dwell in a land of deep darkness, but now on them light has shined. Please multiply their fruit; increase their joy; may they rejoice before You as with joy at the harvest, as those who are glad when they divide great spoil. For the yoke of their burdens, and the staff for their shoulders, and the rod of their oppressors, You have broken as on the day of Midian. For to us a child was born, to them the Son was given; and the government is upon His shoulder, and His name is called Wonderful Counselor, Mighty God, Everlasting Father, Prince of Peace.

My children, let us adore our great Savior! Of the increase of His government and of peace there will be no end. He has established it and upholds it with justice and with righteousness from this time forth and forevermore.

O LORD of hosts, thank You that Your zeal has accomplished salvation for them through Christ. Amen (Isaiah 9).

*In personal relationships, if we attempt to fake emotional intensity and put on an outward show of emotion that is not consistent with the feelings of our hearts, others involved will usually sense our hypocrisy at once and be put off by it. How much more is this true of God, who fully knows our hearts. Therefore, intensity and depth of emotional involvement in prayer should never be faked: we cannot fool God.*
~Wayne Grudem

ajestic One,

In this day let my children lean on You, the Holy One of Israel, in truth. Please continue to change them into the likeness of the shoot that came forth from the stump of Jesse. May Your Spirit rest upon them, the Spirit of wisdom and understanding, the Spirit of counsel and might, the Spirit of knowledge and the fear of the LORD. And let their delight be always in the fear of You. Clothe them with right-eousness as the belt of their waists, and faithfulness as the belt of their loins.

I will give thanks to You, O LORD, for though You were once angry with them, Your anger turned away because of Christ, that You might comfort them.

My children, God is your salvation; trust, and do not be afraid; for the LORD GOD is your strength and your song, and He has become your salvation!

Therefore, O God, cause them to draw water from the wells of salvation with joy. And may they give thanks to You, call upon Your name, make known Your deeds among the peoples, and proclaim that Your name is exalted. May they sing praises to You, for You have done gloriously; let them make this known in all the earth. Let us shout together and sing for joy, for great in our midst are You, O Holy One of Israel (Isaiah 10, 11, 12).

overeign, eternal, unchangeable LORD, You are my God; I will exalt You; I will praise Your name, for You have done wonderful things, plans formed of old, faithful and sure. For You have made my children; they are the work of Your hands. Let them glorify You; let them fear You. May You be to them a stronghold; a stronghold when they are needy and in distress, their shelter from the storm and their shade from the heat.

May they hope and long for the day when You will make for all peoples a feast of rich food, a feast of well-aged wine, of rich food full of marrow, of aged wine well refined.

My children, on that day He will swallow up death forever; and the Lord GOD will wipe away tears from all faces, and the reproach of His people He will take away from all the earth, for the LORD has spoken.

You are our God; we have waited for You, that You might save us. You are the LORD; together we have waited for You; let us be glad and rejoice in Your salvation. Keep them in perfect peace because their minds are stayed on You, because they trust in You. Help them to trust in You forever, for You are an everlasting rock (Isaiah 25 & 26).

---

*You should, in Tertullian's phrase, with a holy conspiracy,*
*besiege heaven.* ~Thomas Manton

LORD my God,
Please make level the path of my children; for You make the way of the righteous level. In the path of Your judgments, O LORD, let them wait for You; may Your name and remembrance be the desire of their souls. Make their souls yearn for You in the night; cause their spirits within them to earnestly seek You. For when Your judgments are in the earth, the inhabitants of the world learn righteousness.

O LORD, ordain peace for them; do for them all their works. Even though other lords besides You may rule over them, let them bring Your name alone to remembrance.

You have made them a pleasant vineyard, a vineyard of wine; I will sing of them! Let them trust You, for You, the LORD, are their keeper; every moment You water them. You keep them night and day; may they lay hold of Your protection. In the days to come let them blossom and put forth shoots and fill the whole world with fruit. Amen (Isaiah 26 & 27).

ORD of power,

Please be to my children a crown of glory and a diadem of beauty. For You are the LORD of hosts, wonderful in counsel and excellent in wisdom.

Protect them from hypocrisy. May it never be that they draw near with their mouths and honor You with their lips, while their hearts are far from You. Let their fear of You be genuine, and not a commandment taught by men.

My children, guard your hearts, lest you turn things upside down and regard the Potter as the clay.

O LORD, keep them from saying of their Maker, "He did not make me"; or of You who formed them, "He has no understanding." Instead, let them be turned into a fruitful field. Out of their gloom and darkness cause them to see and obtain fresh joy in You. May they exult in You, the Holy One of Israel, and no more be ashamed. Let them see the work of Your hands and sanctify Your name; let them sanctify the Holy One of Jacob and stand in awe of the God of Israel (Isaiah 28 & 29).

*Just as God's Word must reform our theology, our ethics, and our practices, so also must it reform our praying.* ~D.A. Carson

xalted Fountain of Grace,
May my children find their strength in quietness
and in trust, for You wait to be gracious to them.
Therefore, exalt Yourself to show mercy to them. For You are
a God of justice; blessed are all those who wait for You.
Gather them into Your arms so that they will weep no more.

My children, He will surely be gracious to you at the
sound of your cry. As soon as He hears it, He answers you.

Let them trust Your promise, O LORD, that though You
give them the bread of adversity and the water of affliction,
yet You will not hide Yourself forever, but their eyes shall see
their Teacher. And may their ears hear a word behind them,
saying, "This is the way, walk in it," when they turn to the
right or when they turn to the left. Let them also defile their
idols of the flesh, and scatter them as unclean things, saying
to them, "Be gone!"

Cause their hope to remain rooted and steadfast in You
when calamity overtakes them. For soon the light of the
moon will be as the light of the sun, and the light of the sun
will be sevenfold, as the light of seven days, in the day when
You bind up the brokenness of Your people, and heal the
wounds inflicted by Your blow. With Your burning anger
devour their enemies, and give them a song as in the night
when a holy feast is kept, and gladness of heart, as when one
sets out to the sound of the flute to go to the mountain of the
LORD, to the Rock of Israel. Cause Your majestic voice to be
heard by them. Amen (Isaiah 30).

orker of wonders,

Continue to make my children righteous, so that they may have peace, quietness, and security forever. O LORD, be gracious to them; I wait for You. Be their arm every morning, their salvation in the time of trouble. For You are exalted, for You dwell on high; fill them with justice and righteousness, and be the stability of their days, abundance of salvation, wisdom, and knowledge; let the fear of You be their treasure. Arise, O LORD, lift Yourself up; be exalted in them.

Help them to become men and women who walk righteously and speak uprightly, who despise the gain of oppressions, who shake their hands, lest they hold a bribe, who stop their ears from hearing of bloodshed and shut their eyes from looking on evil. Then they will dwell on the heights; their place of defense will be the fortress of rocks; their bread will be given them; their water will be sure.

Let their eyes behold You in Your beauty. Be with them in majesty, for You are their judge; You are their lawgiver; You are their king; You will save them (Isaiah 32 & 33).

*One cannot begin to face the real difficulties of the life of prayer and meditation unless one is first perfectly content to be a beginner and really experience himself as one who knows little or nothing and has a desperate need to learn the bare rudiments. Those who think they "know" from the beginning will never, in fact, come to know anything.* ~Thomas Merton

eautiful LORD,

Let my precious children be glad as they look to the day of the Son's return. May they rejoice and blossom like the crocus; let them blossom abundantly and rejoice with joy and singing. And may they long to see Your glory, the majesty of their God. Strengthen their weak hands, and make firm their feeble knees.

My children, be not anxious of heart. Be strong; fear not! Behold, your God will come with vengeance, with the recompense of God. He will come and save you. Then the eyes of the blind shall be opened, and the ears of the deaf unstopped; then shall the lame man leap like a deer, and the tongue of the mute sing for joy.

Prepare them, O LORD, to set foot on the great highway, which shall be called the Way of Holiness; for the unclean shall not pass over it. It shall belong to those who walk on the way; let them not go astray. Let them yearn for that day when the redeemed shall walk there, when the ransomed of the LORD shall return and come to Zion with singing. Everlasting joy shall be upon their heads; they shall obtain gladness and joy, and sorrow and sighing shall flee away (Isaiah 35).

*God can pick sense out of a confused prayer.* ~Richard Sibbes

LORD of hosts, God of Israel, enthroned above the cherubim, You are the God, You alone, of all the kingdoms of the earth; You have made heaven and earth; You have made my children. Incline Your ear, O LORD, and hear; open Your eyes, O LORD, and see; and hear all the words of those who mock You, the living God. Truly, O LORD, there are many who desire to lay waste all the fruit of my children's hands. In their wickedness they have destroyed others and cast their gods into the fire—the work of men's hands, wood and stone. So now, O LORD my God, save them from their hands, that all the kingdoms of the earth may know that You alone are the LORD. Please defend them to save them, for Your own sake.

Please, O LORD, remember them and cause them to walk before You in faithfulness and with whole hearts, and to do what is good in Your sight. May they trust that it is for their welfare when they have great bitterness; let them praise You and hope for Your faithfulness.

My children, in love He has delivered your life from the pit of destruction, for He has cast all your sins behind His back.

Let them thank You, O LORD, as I do this day; let them make known to their children Your faithfulness. For it is You who will save us, and we will play music on stringed instruments all the days of our lives, at the house of the LORD (Isaiah 37 & 38).

onderful God,

Comfort, comfort my dear children. Speak tenderly to them and cry to them that their iniquity is pardoned, that because of Christ they have not received from Your hand double for all their sins. May they wait patiently for the day when Your glory shall be revealed, and all flesh shall see it together, for You have spoken.

My children, all flesh is grass, and all its beauty is like the flower of the field. The grass withers, the flower fades when the breath of the LORD blows on it; surely the people are grass. The grass withers, the flower fades, but the word of our God will stand forever.

Lord GOD, let them behold You coming with might; with Your arm ruling for You. Please tend them like a shepherd; gather them into Your arms; carry them in Your bosom, and gently lead them.

May they worship You as the only one who has measured the waters in the hollow of his hand and marked off the heavens with a span, enclosed the dust of the earth in a measure and weighed the mountains in scales and the hills in a balance. We praise You, for no man has directed Your Spirit or shown You his counsel. Amen (Isaiah 40).

*As highly as Paul values marital obligations, he can envisage a couple self-consciously choosing not to have sex together for a while, so that the time they would have spent pleasing each other sexually will be devoted to prayer. That says something about Paul's valuation of prayer.* ~D. A. Carson

reator of the ends of the earth, Be exalted in Your wisdom and fullness, for You have never needed anyone. Whom did You consult, and who made You understand? Who taught You the path of justice, and taught You knowledge, and showed You the way of understanding? Behold, the nations are like a drop from a bucket, and are accounted as the dust on the scales; behold, You take up the coastlands like fine dust. Lebanon would not suffice for fuel, nor are its beasts enough for a burnt offering. All the nations are as nothing before You, they are accounted by You as less than nothing and emptiness.

Therefore, let my treasured children worship and adore Your greatness, taking comfort that You are powerful and lack nothing.

My children, to whom then will you liken God, or what likeness compare with Him? You have known and heard, and it has been told you from the beginning, that it is He who sits above the circle of the earth, and its inhabitants are like grasshoppers; who stretches out the heavens like a curtain, and spreads them like a tent to dwell in; who brings princes to nothing, and makes the rulers of the earth as emptiness.

O Holy One, to whom then will we compare You, that You should be like him? Lift up our eyes on high to see: You created the stars—You who bring out their host by number, calling them all by name, by the greatness of Your might, and because You are strong in power not one is missing (Isaiah 40).

ou who alone are the true God,

May my children never complain that their way is hidden from You, or that their right is disregarded by their God. Instead, assure them that You are the everlasting God, the Creator of the ends of the earth. Instill within them a steadfast confidence in You, for You do not faint or grow weary; Your understanding is unsearchable. Give power to them when they are faint, and when they have no might increase their strength. Even when they faint and become weary, and when they fall exhausted, let them wait on You. For they who wait for You shall renew their strength; they shall mount up with wings like eagles; they shall run and not be weary; they shall walk and not faint.

Thank You for choosing them, for taking them from the pit, for calling them out of bondage, saying to them, "You are my servant, I have chosen you and not cast you off."

My children, fear not, for He is with you; be not dismayed, for He is your God; He will strengthen, He will help you, He will uphold you with His righteous right hand.

O LORD my God, hold their right hands, and say to them, "Fear not, I am the one who helps you" (Isaiah 40 & 41).

*Intercession is more than specific: it is pondered: it requires us to bear on our heart the burden of those for whom we pray.*
~George A. Buttrick

ing of Jacob,

Defend my priceless children from all who are incensed against them; let them be put to shame and confounded; may those who strive against them be as nothing and perish. Let the evil ones who war against them be as nothing at all.

Fear not, my children! He is the one who helps you; your Redeemer is the Holy One of Israel.

O LORD, let them rejoice in You; in the Holy One of Israel let them glory. When they are poor and needy and seek for water, and there is none, and their tongues are parched with thirst, please answer them; O God of Israel, do not forsake them. Open rivers on the bare heights, and fountains in the midst of the valleys. Make the wilderness a pool of water, and the dry land springs of water for them. Put in their wilderness the cedar, the acacia, the myrtle, and the olive. Set in their desert the cypress, the plane and the pine together, that they may see and know, may consider and understand, that Your hand has done it, the Holy One of Israel has created it.

Increase their souls' delight in Your Servant, whom You uphold, Your chosen, just as Your soul delights in Him. May they hope in Him, for a bruised reed He will not break, and a faintly burning wick He will not quench; He will faithfully bring forth justice. Hasten the day of His return! Amen (Isaiah 41 & 42).

God, the LORD,
who created the heavens and stretched them out,
who spread out the earth and what comes from it,
who gives breath to the people on it and spirit to those who walk in it, reassure my children that You are the LORD, and have called them in righteousness. Take them by the hand and keep them. Conform them to the image of Him who is given as a covenant for the people, a light for the nations, to open the eyes that are blind, to bring out the prisoners from the dungeon, from the prison those who sit in darkness.

My children, pursue Christ! Esteem Christ! Honor His Father, for He is the LORD; that is His name; His glory He gives to no other, nor His praise to carved idols.

Let them sing to You a new song, O LORD, Your praise from the end of the earth. Let them lift up their voices along with the sea, and all that fills it, the coastlands and their inhabitants, the desert and its cities. May they sing for joy, and shout from the top of the mountains. Let them give glory to You, and declare Your praise in the coastlands. For You go out like a mighty man, like a man of war You stir up Your zeal; You cry out, You shout aloud, You show Yourself mighty against Your foes.

Lead them in a way that they do not know, in paths that they have not known please guide them. Turn the darkness before them into light, the rough places into level ground. For these are the things that You do, and You will not forsake them (Isaiah 42).

oly LORD,

Be pleased, for Your righteousness' sake, to magnify Your law and make it glorious through my children. Be exalted, for You created them, You formed them. May they fear not, for You have redeemed them; You have called them by name, they are Yours. When they pass through the waters, please be with them; and through the rivers, let them not overwhelm them; when they walk through fire let them not be burned, and may the flame not consume them. For You are the LORD their God, the Holy One of Israel, their Savior.

My children, because you are precious in His eyes, and honored, and He loves you, He gives men in return for you, peoples in exchange for your life. Fear not, for He is with you. He is the LORD, and besides Him there is no savior.

Let them adore You as the LORD, their Redeemer, their Holy One, the Creator of Israel, their King. Give water to them in the wilderness, rivers when they are in the desert, to give drink to Your chosen sons and daughters, the people whom You formed for Yourself that they might declare Your praise. Thank You that You are He who blots out their transgressions for Your own sake, and You will not remember their sins. For they are Your servants whom You have chosen; You made them and formed them from the womb. Help them, and let them not fear. Pour Your Spirit upon their offspring, and Your blessing on their descendants. Let them spring up among the grass like willows by flowing streams. May one say, "I am the LORD's,' and another write on his hand, "The LORD's," and name himself by the name of Israel (Isaiah 42, 43, 44).

ing and Redeemer of Israel,

Glory be to Your name, for You are the first and You are the last; besides You there is no god. Who is like You? Therefore, let my children not fear, nor be afraid; for You declare what is to come, and what will happen. May they trust in You, for there is no god besides You, there is no Rock; I know not any.

Let them remember that all who fashion idols are nothing, and the things they delight in do not profit, for they are Your servants; You formed them; they are Your servants; let them not be forgotten by You.

My children, He has blotted out your transgressions like a cloud and your sins like mist; cling to Him, for He has redeemed you!

Sing, O heavens, for the LORD has done it; shout, O depths of the earth; break forth into singing, O mountains, O forest, and every tree in it! For You, LORD, have redeemed my children, and will be glorified in them. Through them be pleased to display Your beauty.

May they take comfort and rejoice in the knowledge that You formed them in the womb, that You are the LORD, who made all things, who alone stretched out the heavens, who spread out the earth by Yourself, who frustrates the signs of liars and makes fools of diviners, who turns wise men back and makes their knowledge foolish, who says to the deep, "Be dry; I will dry up your rivers." Let them love and fear You. Amen (Isaiah 44).

ORD God of Israel, who calls His people by name,

    I come before You on behalf of my dearest children because You are the LORD, and there is no other, besides You there is no God. Please equip them to make known Your might, that people may know, from the rising of the sun and from the west, that there is none besides You; You are the LORD, and there is no other. May they tremble and rejoice at the truth that You form light and create darkness. Let them worship and bow down before You as the one who makes well-being and creates calamity. May they exalt You as the LORD who does all these things.

My children, praise and adore Him with me! For He made the earth and created man on it; it was His hands that stretched out the heavens, and He commanded all their host.

Stir them up, O LORD, in righteousness, and make all their ways level. May the wealthy and men of stature come to them, saying, "Surely God is in you, and there is no other, no god besides Him."

Many men make idols and go in confusion together. But I thank You that my children are saved by You with everlasting salvation; they shall not be put to shame or confounded to all eternity. For You are the LORD and there is no other. You did not say to them, "Seek me in vain." You speak truth; You declare what is right (Isaiah 45).

*All progress in prayer is an answer to prayer—our own or another's. And all true prayer promotes its own progress and increases our power to pray.* ~P. T. Forsyth

God who hears prayer, Let my children turn continually to You for their salvation. For You are God, and there is no other. Therefore let them say of You, "Only in the LORD are righteousness and strength." Thank You that in You they are justified and glory. Praise be to Your name, for they have been borne by You from before their birth, carried from the womb; even to their old age You are He, and to gray hairs You will carry them. You have made, and You will bear; You will carry and will save.

My children, remember with me that He is God, and there is no other; He is God, and there is none like Him, declaring the end from the beginning and from ancient times things not yet done, saying, "My counsel shall stand, and I will accomplish all my purpose."

Therefore, great LORD, may they trust the word that goes out from Your mouth in righteousness. Let them hope in You as the God who brings to pass what He speaks; who does what He has purposed. For Your name's sake be gracious to them, for the sake of Your praise make them walk in holiness, and do not cut them off. Refine them, and give them strength as You try them in the furnace of affliction. For Your own sake, for Your own sake, do this, for how should Your name be profaned? Your glory You will not give to another. Therefore magnify Yourself in them! Glorify Yourself through them! Use them to exalt the greatness of Your name. Amen (Isaiah 45, 46, 48).

y Redeemer,

Teach my children to profit from uprightness, and lead them in the way they should go. Make them pay attention to Your commandments so that their peace will be like a river, and their righteousness like the waves of the sea; then let their offspring be like the sand, and their descendents like its grains; may their name never be cut off or destroyed from before You.

Now, even now I shout for joy, for You have redeemed them! Therefore do not let them thirst when You lead them through deserts; make water flow for them even from the rocks, so that their souls are satisfied.

Make their mouths like a sharp sword; in the shadow of Your hand please hide them; make them a polished arrow; in Your quiver hide them away.

My children, you are the LORD's servants, in whom He will be glorified and display His beauty. You have not labored in vain; you have not spent your strength for nothing. For surely your recompense is with your God.

I will praise You, O LORD, for You called them from the womb, from the body of their mother You named their name. You formed them from the womb to be Your servants, therefore may they be honored in Your eyes, and may You continually be their strength. Make them as a light for the nations, that Your salvation may reach to the ends of the earth. Let kings see and arise; may princes prostrate themselves; because of You, who are faithful, the Holy One of Israel, who has chosen them (Isaiah 48 & 49).

uler of heaven and earth,

Please keep my precious children. Answer them and help them; let them not hunger or thirst, and may neither scorching wind nor sun strike them. Have pity on them and lead them, and by springs of water guide them.

Sing for joy, O heavens, and exult, O earth; break forth, O mountains, into singing! for the LORD has comforted my children and will have compassion on their affliction.

I praise You that You have not forsaken them; You have not forgotten them. Even a woman may forget her nursing child, yet You will not forget my children. Assure them of this, and let them know that You are the LORD; those who wait for You shall not be put to shame. Fight for them; contend with those who contend with them. Then all flesh shall know that You are the LORD their Savior, and their Redeemer, the Mighty One of Jacob (Isaiah 49).

*The artless child is still the divine model for all of us. Prayer will increase in power and reality as we repudiate all pretense and learn to be utterly honest before God as well as before men.*
~A. W. Tozer

orgiving God,

Thank You that Your hand is not shortened, that it can redeem my dear children. For by Your power and rebuke You dry up the sea, and make the rivers a desert.

Please give them the tongue of those who are taught, that they may know how to sustain with a word those who are weary. Morning by morning awaken them; awaken their ears to hear as those who are taught.

When they are struck and spit upon for Your namesake fill them with hope in You, the Lord GOD. For You will help them; therefore they will not be disgraced. Remind them that they will not be put to shame, for You who vindicate them are near.

Let them fear You and obey the voice of Your servant, Christ. And when they walk in darkness and have no light let them trust in Your name and rely on their God. Cause them to pursue righteousness and seek You. Make their wilderness like Eden, their desert like the garden of the LORD; may joy and gladness be found in them, thanksgiving and the voice of song (Isaiah 50 & 51).

*Prayer is often represented as the great means of the Christian life. But it is no mere means, it is the great end of that life. It is, of course, not untrue to call it a means. It is so, especially at first. But at last it is truer to say that we live the Christian life in order to pray than that we pray in order to live the Christian life.* ~P. T. Forsyth

ovely God,

Turn the attention of my children to Yourself. Let them give ear to the law that has gone out from You, to the justice that You have set for a light to the peoples. May Your righteousness draw near to them, let Your salvation go out to them; make them hope for You, and for Your arm let them wait.

Lift up their eyes to the heavens, and cause them to look at the earth beneath and see that the heavens vanish like smoke, the earth will wear out like a garment, and they who dwell in it will die in the same way. But remind them that Your salvation will be forever, and Your righteousness will never be dismayed.

Listen to Him, my children, you who know righteousness; for He says, "Fear not the reproach of man, nor be dismayed at their revilings. For the moth will eat them up like a garment, and the worm will eat them like wool; but my righteousness will be forever, and my salvation to all generations."

Awake, awake, put on strength, O arm of the LORD; awake, as in days of old, the generations of long ago, and defend my children. Ransom them, so that they will come into Your presence with singing; crown their heads with everlasting joy; grant them gladness and joy, so that sorrow and sighing shall flee away.

Teach them to not be afraid of man who dies, of the son of man who is made like grass, for You, You are He who comforts them. Let them take confidence in You, their Maker, who stretched out the heavens and laid the foundations of the earth, and may they not fear the oppressors who set themselves up to destroy (Isaiah 51).

ord of the oceans, who stirs up the sea so that its waves roar, please put Your words in my children's mouths and cover them in the shadow of Your hand. For You are the LORD of hosts, who established the heavens and laid the foundations of the earth, and say to them, "You are my sons and daughters."

Thank You for awakening them from the slumber of death, for clothing them with strength and beautiful garments. For they were sold for nothing, and You have redeemed them without money. Therefore make their feet beautiful upon the mountains, as one who brings good news, who publishes peace, who brings good news of happiness, who publishes salvation, who says, "My God reigns." Let them lift up their voices with me, so that together we may sing for joy, and eye to eye await the return of Your Son.

My children, let us break forth together into singing, for the LORD has comforted His people; He has redeemed even us! The LORD has bared His holy arm before the eyes of all the nations, and all the ends of the earth shall see the salvation of our God.

LORD, please go always before them; O God of Israel, be their rear guard. Amen (Isaiah 51 & 52).

*When our awareness of the greatness of God and the gospel is dim, our prayer lives will be small. The less we think of the nature and character of God, and the less we are reminded of what Jesus did for us on the Cross, the less we want to pray.*
~Donald S. Whitney

y Father and my God,

Grow within the hearts of my wonderful children a deep esteem for Him who has borne their griefs and carried their sorrows, who was wounded for their transgressions and crushed for their iniquities. May they treasure Him increasingly, desire Him more fervently, for upon Him was the chastisement that brought their peace, and with His stripes they are healed.

Let them love and cherish Him as the One stricken for their transgression. May they praise You with trembling for crushing Him so that they could be accounted righteous. Stir up gratitude within them for His sacrifice, for bearing their iniquities, pouring out His soul to death, and for making intercession for them.

Sing, My children! Break forth into singing and cry aloud! For you have been reconciled to your Maker and Husband, to the LORD of hosts; the Holy of One of Israel is your Redeemer!

O LORD, thank You for calling them when they were like children deserted and grieved in spirit. And now be exalted for Your great compassion toward them! Keep them in Your sovereign arms. Amen (Isaiah 53 & 54).

od of the whole earth,

Do not hide Your beautiful face from my children or be angry with them, but with everlasting love have compassion on them. Even though the mountains may depart and the hills be removed, let not Your steadfast love depart from them, and do not remove Your covenant of peace, but continue to have compassion on them.

My children, although you may be afflicted and storm-tossed, take comfort in His word! For behold, He will set your stones in antimony, and lay your foundations with sapphires. He will wall you in with precious stones.

LORD, bless them, and may all their children be taught by You, and let the peace of their children be great. Establish them in righteousness; keep them far from oppression and fear. Protect them from terror; may it not come near them. I commit them to Your hand, for You are able to guard them so that no weapon that is fashioned against them shall succeed (Isaiah 54).

*Meditation is a middle sort of duty between the word and prayer, and hath respect to both. The word feedeth meditation, and meditation feedeth prayer. These duties must always go hand in hand; meditation must follow hearing and precede prayer. To hear and not to meditate is unfruitful. We may hear and hear, but it is like putting a thing into a bag with holes.... It is rashness to pray and not to meditate. What we take in by the word we digest by meditation and let out by prayer. These three duties must be ordered that one may not jostle out the other. Men are barren, dry, and sapless in their prayers for want of exercising themselves in holy thoughts.* ~ Thomas Manton

ompassionate LORD,

When my children thirst, draw them to the waters, draw them to Yourself. Keep them from spending their money for that which is not bread, and their labor for that which does not satisfy. Instead, make them listen diligently to You, and eat what is good, and delight themselves in rich food—wine and milk without price. Incline their ears, and let them come to You; may they hear, that their souls may live, because of Your everlasting covenant of steadfast, sure love.

My children, seek the LORD while He may be found; call upon Him while He is near! Let us forsake our wicked ways and our unrighteous thoughts; and let us turn to the LORD, that He may have compassion on us, and to our God, for He will abundantly pardon.

Holy One of Israel, we bow together before You, for Your thoughts are not our thoughts, neither are Your ways our ways. We worship and exalt You, for as the heavens are higher than the earth, so are Your ways higher than our ways and Your thoughts than our thoughts. Amen (Isaiah 55).

ou who are high and lifted up,

Be pleased to fill my treasured children with joy and lead them forth in peace. May they keep justice, and do righteousness, for Your salvation has come, and Your deliverance is revealed. Keep their hands from doing any evil, and make them hold on to righteousness.

Thank You for saving them; for giving them an everlasting name that shall not be cut off. Let the mountains and the hills break forth into singing, and all the trees of the field clap their hands! For You have made a name for Yourself; You have redeemed them! Make them joyful in Your house of prayer.

Please protect them from blind watchmen without knowledge, from shepherds who have no understanding. Revive their spirits when they are lowly, and revive their hearts when they are contrite. May they seek You daily and delight to know Your ways; let them delight to draw near to You. And when they fast, may it not be merely to quarrel and pursue their own business. But cause them to fast as You choose: to loose the bonds of wickedness, to undo the straps of the yoke, to let the oppressed go free, to share their bread with the hungry, to bring the homeless poor into their houses, and to clothe the naked. Then may their light break forth like the dawn, and make righteousness go before them, with Your glory as their rear guard (Isaiah 55, 56, 58).

*A chief object of all prayer is to bring us to God....*
*The chief failure of prayer is its cessation.* ~P. T. Forsyth

ou who inhabit eternity,
When I call to You, please answer. I cry out to You
on behalf of my dearest children. Keep them from
speaking wickedness. But rather, may they pour themselves
out for the hungry and satisfy the desire of the afflicted, for
then shall their light rise in the darkness and their gloom be
as the noonday. Guide them continually and satisfy their
desire in scorched places and make their bones strong; may
they be like a watered garden, like a spring of water, whose
waters do not fail. Let them take delight in You; feed them
with the heritage of Jacob.

My children, arise, shine, for your light has come, and the
glory of the LORD has risen upon you. Although darkness
once covered you, now the LORD has risen upon you, and His
glory is seen upon you. And nations shall come to your light,
and kings to the brightness of Christ in you!

LORD God, may peoples see them and be radiant; let their
hearts thrill and exult because of the abundance of their joy
in Christ. Make them declare the good news—the praises of
Christ. Beautify your servants so that the coastlands will hope
for You, for the name of the LORD their God, and for the Holy
One of Israel, because You have made them beautiful (Isaiah
58 & 60).

God whose name is Holy,

In Your favor be pleased to have mercy on my beautiful children. Make them majestic forever, and a joy to every age, so that all may know that You, the LORD, are their Savior and their Redeemer, the Mighty One of Jacob. Make their overseers peace and their taskmasters righteousness. May their walls be called Salvation, and the gates to their houses Praise.

My children, trust in the LORD, and He will be your everlasting light, and your God will be your glory! Seek His face, and He will be your beauty.

LORD, let them hope in You as their everlasting light. Clothe them with righteousness that You may be glorified. Use them to display Your beauty.

Please comfort them when they mourn; give them the oil of gladness instead of mourning, the garment of praise instead of a faint spirit; that they may be called oaks of righteousness, the planting of the LORD, that You may be glorified. Let them greatly rejoice in You; let their souls exult in their God, for You have clothed them with the garments of salvation; You have covered them with the robe of righteousness, as a bride adorns herself with her jewels. As the earth brings forth its sprouts, and as a garden causes what is sown in it to sprout up, so cause righteousness and praise to sprout up before them. Amen (Isaiah 60 & 61).

*Even as the moon influences the tides of the sea, even so does prayer...influence the tides of godliness. ~Charles Spurgeon*

uthor of all existence,

For my wonderful children's sake do not keep silent, and for their sake do not be quiet, until their righteousness goes forth as brightness, and their salvation as a burning torch. Let men see their righteousness, and women their glory, because You have called them by a new name that Your mouth has given. May they be as a crown of beauty in Your hand, and a royal diadem in the hand of their God. Let them be called My Delight Is in Them, for You delight in Your servants. Fill them with the joyful knowledge that You take pleasure in them, that as the bridegroom rejoices over the bride, so You rejoice over them. Please establish them and make them a praise in the earth. Let those who eat the grain and drink the wine of their houses praise the LORD, and exult in Your holiness.

My children, behold, your salvation has come; behold, His reward is Himself! Rejoice! For you are numbered among The Holy People, The Redeemed of the LORD; and you are called Sought Out, A Child Not Forsaken.

O Mighty One, help them to put their hope in You—You who are splendid in Your apparel, marching in the greatness of Your strength, speaking in righteousness, mighty to save. Thank You for sparing their lifeblood and bringing to them salvation by Your powerful arm. Thank You, that when they deserved to be trod in Your anger and trampled in Your wrath, You gave Christ to bear their punishment! We bless His name together, for He is our joy and our salvation (Isaiah 62 & 63).

ource of all blessedness,
Let my children be men and women who recount Your steadfast love, Your praises, according to all that You have given us, and the great goodness to our house that You have granted us according to Your compassion, according to the abundance of Your steadfast love. Thank You for becoming their Savior; that in Your love and in Your pity You have redeemed them, and lifted them up and carried them. Please continue to lead them, to make for Yourself a glorious name.

My children, it is my joy once again to remind you that He is your Father, though Abraham does not know you; He, the LORD, is your Father, your Redeemer from of old is His name!

O LORD, do not make them wander from Your ways and harden their hearts, so that they fear You not. Keep them, and let them wait for You. For from of old no one has heard or perceived by the ear, no eye has seen a God besides You, who acts for those who wait for Him. You meet them who joyfully work righteousness—they who remember Your ways. Therefore may they present themselves to You as joyful servants of righteousness, remembering the ways of their God (Isaiah 63 & 64).

raiseworthy LORD,

I am glad and rejoice forever in my children whom You have created; for behold, You made their faces to be my joy, and their presence to be my gladness. Give them the assurance that You also rejoice in them and are glad in Your people.

Let them live by faith, hoping for the day when You create a new heavens and a new earth—when the sound of weeping and the cry of distress shall be heard no more, when Your chosen shall not labor in vain or bear children for calamity, when the wolf and the lamb shall graze together.

Guard them from the subtle deceitfulness of pride; help them to fight against arrogance. For these are the ones to whom You will look: they who are humble and contrite in spirit and tremble at Your word.

Let them see Your glory and declare it among the nations, so that all flesh may know that You are the LORD and come to worship before You (Isaiah 65 & 66).

*Joy and prayer belong together. Paul thought so when he wrote, "Be joyful always; pray continually; give thanks in all circumstances, for this is God's will for you in Christ Jesus" (I Thessalonians 5:16-18). Many Christians have wondered how it's possible to "pray continually," but not many notice the words immediately preceding: "Be joyful always." We're more familiar with the call to prayer than with the call to joy. We know the saying, "God loves a cheerful giver" (2 Corinthians 9:7), but do we realize He also loves a cheerful pray-er?*
*~Mike Mason*

nfinitely worthy LORD,

I will sing to You, for You have done glorious things; You have made my children, You made Yourself their strength and their song, and You have become their salvation! You are my God, and I will praise You for them; You are the God of Jacob, and I will exalt You. Your right hand, O LORD, glorious in power, Your right hand, O LORD, shatters their enemies. In the greatness of Your majesty You overthrow their adversaries; You send out Your fury; it consumes them like stubble.

Who is like You, O LORD, among the gods? Who is like You, majestic in holiness, awesome in glorious deeds, doing wonders? You have led in Your steadfast love my children whom You have redeemed; You have guided them by Your strength to Your holy abode. You alone will reign forever and ever.

I will sing to You, for You have triumphed gloriously over their enemies; You will guard and defend them, for You have become their salvation! (Exodus 15).

*What is the reason that some believers are so much brighter and holier than others? I believe the difference, nineteen cases out of twenty, arises from different habits about private prayer. I believe that those who are not eminently holy pray little, and those who are eminently holy pray much.* ~J. C. Ryle

ost blessed Lord,

Let my children be men and women who proclaim Your name and ascribe greatness to their God. For You are the Rock, whose work is perfect, for all Your ways are justice. A God of faithfulness and without iniquity, just and upright are You.

Keep them from becoming unmindful of the Rock that bore them, from forgetting the God who gave them birth. But make them remember and rejoice that You, even You, are their help, and there is no god beside You. You kill and You make alive; You wound and You heal; and there is none that can deliver out of Your hand.

Rejoice with Him, My children; bow down to Him, for He avenges the blood of His children and takes vengeance on His adversaries.

Most High God, let them dwell in safety; surround them all day long, and dwell between their shoulders. May they be blessed by You with favor, and be full of the blessing of the LORD. For there is none like You, who ride through the heavens to their help, through the skies in Your majesty. Be their dwelling place, and keep Your everlasting arms underneath them. Amen (Deuteronomy 32 & 33).

Lord GOD,
Who am I, and what is my house, that You have given me such marvelous children? And yet this was a small thing in Your eyes, O Lord GOD. According to Your own heart You have brought them to me, to make Your servant know Your abundant goodness. Therefore You are great, O LORD God. For there is none like You, and there is no God besides You.

Establish them for Yourself to be Yours forever. And You, O LORD, become their God.

And now, O LORD God, let Your name be magnified forever through them. Let them say, "The LORD of hosts is God over His people." Your promises are sure, therefore Your servant has found courage to pray this prayer to You. May it please You to bless the children of Your servant, so that they may continue forever before You. For only with Your blessing shall the children of Your servant be blessed forever (II Samuel 7).

*The great fault of the children of God is, they do not continue in prayer; they do not go on praying; they do not persevere. If they desire anything for God's glory, they should pray until they get it. Oh, how good, and kind, and gracious, and condescending is the One with Whom we have to do! He has given me, unworthy as I am, immeasurably above all I had asked or thought!*
~George Mueller

ORD of Thunder,
Please be my dear children's rock and their
fortress and their deliverer, their God, their rock,
in whom they take refuge, their shield, and the horn of their
salvation, their stronghold and their refuge, their Savior; save
them from violence. I call upon You, who are worthy to be
praised, to plead for their perseverance.

When the waves of death encompass them, when the
torrents of destruction assail them, let them hope in You.
When the cords of Sheol entangle them, when the snares of
death confront them, in their distress let them call upon You;
may they call to their God. Hear their voices, and may their
cry come to Your ears. Send from on high and take hold of
them; draw them out of many waters. Rescue them and bring
them out into a broad place; rescue them because You delight
in them.

Enable them to keep Your ways and let them not wickedly
depart from their God. May all Your rules be before them,
and from Your statutes may they not turn aside. Make them
blameless before You, and help them to keep themselves
from guilt. Mold them into merciful, pure men and women,
for with the merciful You show Yourself merciful; with the
blameless man and woman You show Yourself blameless;
with the purified You deal purely, and with the crooked You
make Yourself seem tortuous (II Samuel 22).

avior of a humble people,
Be my children's lamp, O LORD, and lighten their darkness. Lead them in Your way, for Your way is perfect; Your word proves true; be a shield for them as they take refuge in You. For who is God but You? And who is a rock, except You? Therefore please be their strong refuge and make their way blameless. Make their feet like the feet of a deer and set them securely on the heights. Train their hands for war, so that they may use the shield of Your salvation.

By Your gentleness make them great. Give a wide place for their steps under them, and let their feet not slip. Equip them with strength for battle; make the evil that rises against them sink under them.

My children, the LORD lives, and blessed be our rock, and exalted be our God, the rock of our salvation!

For this we will praise You, O LORD, among the nations, and sing praises to Your name! Bring great salvation to my children, and show steadfast love to them forever (II Samuel 22).

*The prayerless spirit saps a people's moral strength because it blunts their thought and conviction of the Holy. It must be so if prayer is such a moral blessing and such a shaping power, if it pass, by its nature, from the vague volume and passion of devotion to formed petition and effort. Prayerlessness is an injustice and a damage to our own soul, and therefore to its history, both in what we do and what we think. The root of all deadly heresy is prayerlessness.* ~P. T. Forsyth

od of Jacob,
Raise up my children to live in the fear of You, so that they may dawn on their own children like the morning light, like the sun shining forth on a cloudless morning, like rain that makes grass to sprout from the earth.

Thank You that You have shown great and steadfast love to them, and have caused them to walk before You in faithfulness, in righteousness, and in uprightness of heart toward You. Please keep for them this great and steadfast love.

Give them understanding minds that they may discern between good and evil. Grant them wise and discerning minds, so that they may walk in Your ways, keeping Your statutes and Your commandments. For there is no God like You, O LORD, in heaven above or on earth beneath, keeping covenant and showing steadfast love to Your servants who walk before You with all their hearts. Behold, heaven and the highest heaven cannot contain You, yet have regard to the prayer of Your servant and my plea, O LORD, my God, listening to the cry and to the prayer that Your servant prays before You this day on behalf of my children. Let them fear You all the days that they live, and may they shine forth the greatness of Your name, Your mighty hand, and Your outstretched arm (II Samuel 23, I Kings 3, 8).

*There are many good resources for learning how to pray, but the best way to learn how to pray is to pray.* ~Donald Whitney

ock of Israel,

There is no God like You, in heaven above or on earth beneath, keeping covenant and steadfast love to Your servants who walk before You with all their heart. Therefore I ask that You would incline the hearts of my dearest children to walk in Your ways, keeping Your statutes. Keep them in the way everlasting; let them pay close attention to their way, to walk before You as David walked before You. Listen to the plea of Your servant when I pray for them; hear from heaven and teach them the good way in which they should walk, and rain grace upon them that they may fear You all the days of their lives.

Let Your eyes be open to their pleas, giving ear to them whenever they call You. For You chose them from among all the people of the earth to be Your heritage.

Blessed are You, O LORD, who has given rest to my children. Not one word has failed of all Your good promise, which You spoke to Moses Your servant, which is theirs in Christ Jesus! Be with them, and do not leave them or forsake them, that You may incline their hearts to Yourself, to walk in all Your ways and to keep Your commandments, Your statutes, and Your rules. Maintain their cause, that all the peoples of the earth may know that the LORD is God; there is no other. Let their hearts therefore be wholly true to You our God, walking in Your statutes and keeping Your commandments (I Kings 8).

LORD the God of Israel,
Who is enthroned above the cherubim,
You are the God, You alone, of all the kingdoms of the earth; You have made heaven and earth. Incline Your ear, O LORD, and hear; open Your eyes, O LORD, and see; and hear the words of my prayer on behalf of my children.

Let them give thanks to You; let them call upon Your name and make known Your deeds among the peoples! May they sing to You; let them sing praises to You and tell of all Your wonderful works! Cause them to glory in Your holy name; let their hearts seek You and rejoice!

My children, chosen of Jacob, seek the LORD and His strength; seek His presence continually! Remember the wondrous works that He has done, His miracles and judgments He uttered.

LORD God, help them to remember Your covenant forever, the word that You commanded, for a thousand generations, the covenant that You made with Abraham. Let them sing to You with all the earth and tell of Your salvation from day to day! May they declare Your glory among the nations, Your marvelous works among all the peoples! For great are You, O LORD, and greatly to be praised, and You are to be held in awe above all gods. For all the gods of the peoples are idols, but You made the heavens. Splendor and majesty are before You; strength and joy are in Your place (II Kings 19 & I Chronicles 16).

od of my salvation,

Please increase my children's desire to ascribe to You glory and strength—to ascribe to You the glory due Your name and come humbly before You! Let them worship You in the splendor of holiness, trembling before You with joy. Let them be glad with the heavens, and rejoice with the earth, and let them say among the nations, "The LORD reigns!" Let them roar with the sea, and all that fills it; let them exult with the field, and everything in it! Then make them sing for joy with the trees of the forest before You, for You come to judge the earth.

My children, give thanks to the LORD, for He is good; for His steadfast love endures forever.

Keep them to the end, O God of our salvation, and deliver them from among the nations, that they may give thanks to Your holy name, and glory in Your praise. For blessed are You, the God of Israel, from everlasting to everlasting! Amen. Praise the LORD! (I Chronicles 16).

*The opposite of planning is the rut. If you don't plan a vacation you will probably stay home and watch TV. The natural, unplanned flow of spiritual life sinks to the lowest ebb of vitality. There is a race to be run and a fight to be fought. If you want renewal in your life of prayer you must plan to see it.*
~John Piper.

ord of all being,

Let Your eyes be open and Your ears attentive to the prayer of Your servant. And now arise, O LORD, and go to my children. Clothe them with salvation, and make them rejoice in Your goodness. Remember Your steadfast love for my precious children. Let them worship You and give thanks to You, saying, "For He is good, for His steadfast love endures forever."

May they continually humble themselves, and pray and seek Your face and turn from wicked ways. Open Your eyes and let Your ears be attentive to them, for You have chosen and consecrated them that Your name may be exalted forever. Let them praise You as the God of heaven, who rules over all the kingdoms of the nations—as the God in whose hand are power and might, so that none is able to withstand You. May they give thanks to You, for Your steadfast love endures forever (II Chronicles 6 & 20).

y God, the great, the mighty, and the awesome God, O that my children would delight themselves in Your great goodness! Thank You that even when they forget You and stray from Your commandments, in Your great mercies You do not make an end of them or forsake them, for You are a gracious and merciful God.

When hardships befall them, let them not seem little to You; when they cry to You hear from heaven and deliver them according to Your mercies.

Be exalted in Your grace, for although we have acted wickedly, You have dealt faithfully.

Let them not boast in their wisdom, nor in their might, nor in their riches, but let them boast in this: that they understand and know You, that You are the LORD who practices steadfast love, and justice, and righteousness in the earth. For in these things You delight.

There is none like You, O LORD; You are great, and Your name is great in might. May they fear You, O King of the nations. For this is Your due; for among all the wise ones of the nations and in all their kingdoms there is none like You (Nehemiah 9, Jeremiah 9 & 10).

*As it is the business of tailors to make clothes and of cobblers to mend shoes, so it is the business of Christians to pray.*
~Martin Luther

ternal God,

Let my precious children rejoice in the Word, through whom all things were made. May they seek life only in Him.

Praise be to Your name for causing them to receive Him and believe on His name, for giving them the right to become Your children. Open their eyes to the glory of the Word, the glory of Your only Son, full of grace and truth. From His fullness let them receive grace upon grace—the grace and truth that come through Jesus Christ. Help them to do what is true and come to the light, so that it may be clearly seen that their deeds have been carried out in You.

Help them not to judge by appearances, but instead to judge with right judgment. And when they thirst, let them go to Christ and drink. Let them follow closely after Him always, so that they will not walk in darkness, but will have the light of life. Make them abide in His word as true disciples so that they may know the truth and be set free by it (John 1 & 8).

reat Life-Giver,

May my wonderful children never faint in following after their Shepherd's voice. Let Christ go before them and lead them, calling them by name and wooing them with His words.

Let them flee from the stranger, from the thief, and from the robber, for they do not know their voice.

I praise You that they have entered by Your Son into salvation and plentiful pasture. May they have life and have it abundantly in Him, for that is why He came. Let them trust Him always as their good Shepherd who lays down His life for sheep like them.

Enable me to shepherd them as Christ does, to lay my own life down for them, to guard and guide them diligently. May I never be like the hired hand who sees the wolf coming and leaves them and flees.

My children, trust Christ as your Shepherd! For His Father, who has given you to Him, is greater than all, and no one is able to snatch you out of Your Father's hand. And Christ and the Father are one (John 10).

*Nothing would do more to cure us of a belief in our own wisdom than the granting of some of our eager prayers. And nothing could humiliate us more than to have God say when the fulfillment of our desire brought leanness to our souls, "Well, you would have it." It is what He has said to many. But He has said more, "My grace is sufficient for thee."*
~P. T. Forsyth

lmighty Father,
Stir within my dear children a stronger desire to glorify the Son of Man. Let them seek to glorify Him even in their death. For unless a grain of wheat falls into the earth and dies, it remains alone; but if it dies, it bears much fruit. And my desire is that they bear much fruit for the splendor of Your name. Therefore let them not love their lives and so lose them, but help them to hate their lives in this world so that they may keep them for eternal life. May they serve Christ and follow Christ, for then You will honor them.

Even in this very hour, Father, glorify Your name in them. Draw them to Yourself and let Christ always be their light, that they may not walk in darkness. Let them believe in the light and so become sons and daughters of light. Do not blind their eyes or harden their hearts so that they cannot believe. But in grace shine into their souls and cause them to love the glory that comes from You more than the glory that comes from man (John 12).

ather of our Lord and Teacher,

Please deliver my children from the treachery that still indwells them, for if You remove Your hand of grace they will surely betray Your Son. O spare them that dreadful end! Keep them faithful and steadfast in Jesus all their days, so that He may be glorified, and You will be glorified in Him.

Cause us to grow in love for one another—to strive wholeheartedly to love each other just as Christ has loved us, so that all people will know that we are His disciples, if we have love for one another.

My children, let not your hearts be troubled! Believe in God; believe also in Christ.

Father, fill them afresh with hope for the time when Your Son will come again and will take them to Himself, that where He is they may be also (John 13 & 14).

*Prayer is a special exercise of faith. Faith makes the prayer acceptable because it believes that either the prayer will be answered, or that something better will be given instead.*
~Martin Luther

uthor of Pleasure,

All thanks and praise belong to You for showing my winsome children the way to Yourself, which is through Jesus alone. Blessed be Your glorious name for revealing Christ to them as the way, and the truth, and the life! May they grow to know Him better today than they did yesterday, which is to know You, His Father. I ask this only in Your Son's name, that You may be glorified in Him.

Create within them deeper love for Christ, and let this love constrain them to keep His commandments. Thank You for giving them another Helper to be with them forever, even the Spirit of truth, whom the world cannot receive, because it neither sees Him nor knows Him. Let them sing praise to You, for Your Spirit dwells in them.

My children, do not despair, for Christ has not left us as orphans; He will come to us.

Father, may they love Christ and keep His words. By Your Holy Spirit, teach them all things and bring to their remembrance all that Christ has spoken. Grant His peace to them. Amen (John 14).

overeign Vinedresser,

Let not my precious children's hearts be troubled, neither let them be afraid. Remind them that Christ is mighty to save, and You will not leave them or forsake them. Help them to do as You have commanded them, so that the world may know that they love You.

Please make them branches that bear fruit because they abide in the vine, which is Christ. Prune them, that they may bear more fruit. Preserve them as those who abide in Christ and He in them, so that they bear much fruit, for apart from Christ they can do nothing.

My children, let us abide always in Jesus, with His words abiding in us. For then, when we ask whatever we wish, it will be done for us.

Father, glorify Yourself by making them bear much fruit, and so proving them to be Christ's disciples. May they abide in His love, for as You have loved Him, so has He loved them. Cause them to keep His commandments, for then they will abide in His love, just as He abides in Your love by keeping Your commandments.

Come quickly, Lord Jesus. Amen (John 14 & 15).

*Humbly I asked of God to give me joy,*
*To crown my life with blossoms of delight;*
*I pled for happiness without alloy,*
*Desiring that my pathway should be bright;*
*Prayerfully I sought these blessings to attain, —*
*And now I thank him that he gave me pain....*

*For with the pain and sorrow came to me*
*A dower of tenderness in act and thought;*
*And with the failure came a sympathy,*
*An insight that success had never bought.*
*Father, I had been foolish and unblest*
*If thou had granted me my blind request!*

~L. M. Montgomery

lecting God,

Thank You for choosing my lovely children and appointing them that they should go and bear fruit and that their fruit should abide. How gracious You are to call them Your friends! Fill them with love for their brothers and sisters in Christ, and for me. And fill me with fresh, fervent, bright, divinely-wrought love for them.

If the world hates them, remind them that it hated Christ before it hated them. Prepare them to expect the world's hatred, for You chose them out of the world and they are no longer of the world. Help them to remember the word spoken by Christ: "A servant is not greater than his master," so that they will not be surprised or lose heart when persecution comes.

Let them persevere in bearing witness about Your glorious Son and enable them to do so by Your wonderful Helper, the Spirit of truth, who proceeds from You. May they herald the name of Jesus with boldness and joy.

In the midst of persecution, Father, keep them from falling away! May their hearts not falter in unbelief (John 15).

agnificent Father,

Now that Your Spirit of truth has come, let Him guide my children into all the truth. May He glorify the Son by taking what is Christ's and declaring it to them. When they are sorrowful, turn their sorrow into joy. Fill them with hope that they will see Christ again soon, and then their hearts will rejoice and no one will take their joy from them. Give them confidence to ask things of You in the name of Christ, for then they will receive, that their joy may be full. Imbue their souls with joy in Jesus! Cause them to listen to His words, that in Him they may have peace.

My children, in the world you will have tribulation. But take heart; Christ has overcome the world!

Father, grant them to know You, the only true God, and Jesus Christ more deeply, for that is eternal life. Enable them to glorify You on earth and accomplish the work that You have given them to do. Holy Father, keep them in Your name, that they may be one, even as You and Christ are one. Guard them so that they may never be lost. Open their ears to the words spoken by Your Son that they may have His joy fulfilled in themselves. Thank You for giving us Your word through Christ! Amen (John 16 & 17).

*O what peace we often forfeit,*
*O what needless pain we bear,*
*All because we do not carry*
*Everything to God in prayer!*
~Joseph Scriven

od and Father of my Lord Jesus Christ,
Praise be to Your name because You have blessed my dear children in Christ with every spiritual blessing in the heavenly places, even as You chose them in Him before the foundation of the world, that they should be holy and blameless before You. Please continue to sanctify them by the love with which You predestined them for adoption through Jesus Christ, according to the purpose of Your will, to the praise of Your glorious grace, with which You have blessed them in the Beloved. Worthy is He! How beautiful is Your Son! Let His name be exalted! For in Him they have redemption through His blood, the forgiveness of their trespasses, according to the riches of Your grace, which You lavished on them, in all wisdom and insight.

My children, let us laud His name together for His rich and lavish grace toward us! For in Christ we have obtained an inheritance, having been predestined according to the purpose of Him who works all things according to the counsel of His will, so that we who hope in Christ might be to the praise of His glory!

Father, remind them of their former state as children of wrath by nature, like the rest of mankind, when they were dead in their trespasses and sins. Remind them of this so that they will rejoice afresh that You, being rich in mercy, because of the great love with which You loved them, even when they were dead in their trespasses, made them alive with Christ and saved them by grace. Continue showing them the immeasurable riches of Your grace in kindness toward them in Christ Jesus. Amen (Ephesians 1 & 2).

ighty God,

Thank You for saving my children by pure grace, so that they cannot boast as if it were their own doing, for their salvation is a gift of You and not a result of works. I praise Your name alone for the inestimable treasure that I have in them, because they are Your workmanship, created in Christ Jesus for good works. Therefore assist them to walk in the good works which You prepared beforehand for them.

Remind them constantly that they were at one time separated from Christ, having no hope and without God in the world. Remind them, so that they may rejoice continually that now in Christ Jesus they have been brought near by His blood. Fill them with the confidence that comes from knowing that Christ Himself is their peace—that He has reconciled them to You through the cross. Let them sing for joy anew because He has broken down the dividing wall of hostility between them and You—the one true and holy God.

In Christ please continue building us together into a dwelling place for Yourself by the Spirit. Amen (Ephesians 2).

*No tongue can express, no mind can reach, the heavenly placidness and soul-satisfying delight which are intimated in these words [Eph 2:18]. To come to God as a Father, through Christ, by the help and assistance of the Holy Spirit, revealing him as a Father unto us, and enabling us to go to him as a Father, how full of sweetness and satisfaction is it!*
~John Bunyan

od of revealed mystery,
O that my children would be granted insight into the mystery of Christ by Your Spirit! Give them more and more depth of understanding of this marvelous mystery—that in Christ, through the gospel, they are fellow heirs with the commonwealth of Israel, members of His body, and partakers of the promise. By the working of Your power give them much grace to minister to those in need. Grant them more grace to love and spread the unsearchable riches of Christ, and to bring to light for many what is the plan of the mystery hidden for ages in You who created all things. Through them make known Your manifold wisdom.

Empower them to walk in a manner worthy of the calling to which they have been called, with all humility and gentleness, with patience, bearing with others in love, eager to maintain the unity of the Spirit in the bond of peace. Keep enlarging their hearts and minds with the knowledge of Your Son, unto maturity, to the measure of the stature of the fullness of Christ, so that they may not remain as children, tossed to and fro by the waves and carried about by every wind of doctrine. Guard them from human cunning, from craftiness in deceitful schemes. Enable them to speak the truth in love, to grow up in every way into Him who is the head, into Christ, and to work properly as members of His body, helping to build it up in love (Ephesians 2 & 3).

ondescending God,
Prevent my wonderful children from walking as the world does, in the futility of their minds. Do not let them live as those darkened in their understanding, hard of heart, callous, or greedy to practice every kind of impurity.

Instead, help them to put off their old selves, which are corrupt through deceitful desires. Renew them in the spirit of their minds, and empower them to put on the new self, created after Your likeness in true righteousness and holiness. Make them put away falsehood and speak the truth with their neighbor.

When they are angry keep them from sin; grant them the grace to not let the sun go down on their anger. Let no corrupting talk come out of their mouths, but only such as is good for building up, as fits the occasion, that it may give grace to those who hear. And let them not grieve Your Holy Spirit, by whom they were sealed for the day of redemption. Put all bitterness and wrath and anger and clamor and slander away from them, along with all malice.

Grow us in kindness toward one another, make us tenderhearted, so that we may be always forgiving each other as You forgave us in Christ. Amen (Ephesians 4).

*The first reason why prayer leads to fullness of joy is that prayer is the nerve center of our fellowship with Jesus. He is not here physically to see. But in prayer we speak to Him just as though He were. And in the stillness of those sacred times, we listen to His Word and we pour out to Him our longings.*
~John Piper

ather of glory,

Assist my children to be imitators of You, as Your beloved sons and daughters. And make them walk in love, as Christ loved us and gave Himself up for us, a fragrant offering and sacrifice to You.

Keep them from any form or appearance of sexual immorality and all impurity or covetousness. And may they guard their tongues, so that there might not be any filthiness or foolish talk or crude joking, which are out of place, but instead make them abound with thanksgiving.

Guide their feet to walk as children of light, and enable them to discern what is pleasing to You. Let them take no part in the unfruitful works of darkness, but instead expose them. Open their eyes to look carefully how they walk, not as unwise but as wise, making the best use of the time, because the days are evil. Therefore help them to understand what Your will is.

Fill us together with Your Spirit so that we may address one another in psalms and hymns and spiritual songs, singing and making melody to You with all of our hearts, giving thanks always and for everything to You in the name of our Lord Jesus Christ. And it is in His name that I come to You with this plea for grace. Amen (Ephesians 5).

overeign LORD,

Shall we receive good from You, and shall we not receive evil? Therefore may my precious children hold fast to their integrity when calamity comes. Instead of cursing, let them bless You, saying, "The LORD gave, and the LORD has taken away; blessed be the name of the LORD." When evil befalls them, let them not charge You with wrong or sin with their lips. And when their suffering is great, enable me to comfort them in wisdom and in righteousness.

May they seek You, and to You may they commit their cause. For You do great things and unsearchable, marvelous things without number: You set on high those who are lowly, and those who mourn are lifted up to safety. You save the needy from the sword of the mouth of the crafty and from the hand of the mighty.

Children, behold, your God is faithful when He wounds and shatters you even in your blamelessness. Therefore, do not despise His hard hand of grace, for He binds up, and His hands heal.

Father, deliver my children from troubles! In famine redeem them from death, and in war from the power of the sword! Hide them from the lash of the tongue, and let them not fear destruction when it comes! (Job 1, 2, 4, 5).

⊙≻⊂

*As prayer without faith is but a beating of the air, so trust without prayers [is] but a presumptuous bravado. He that promises to give, and bids us trust his promises, commands us to pray, and expects obedience to his commands. He will give, but not without our asking.* ~Thomas Lye

erciful Almighty,

I am but of yesterday and know nothing, for my days on earth are a shadow. Therefore give wisdom to your servant and deal kindly with me that I might live uprightly with the precious children You have given me. Please fill their mouths with laughter, and their lips with shouting. Let those who hate them be clothed with shame, for You are wise in heart and mighty in strength. You command the sun, and it does not rise; You seal up the stars; You alone stretched out the heavens and trampled the waves of the sea; You made the Bear and Orion, the Pleiades and the chambers of the south; You do great things beyond searching out, and marvelous things beyond number.

O how greatly and marvelously You have made my children! And what a great marvel that You have saved them and kept them with the strength of Your right hand! Praise and glory are due Your name, for You have provided an arbiter between them and Yourself, even the man Jesus Christ, so that You have taken Your rod away from them, and Your dread no longer terrifies them. Therefore may they never loathe their lives, or speak in bitterness of soul, for behold, they have an advocate with You, Jesus Christ the righteous (Job 8, 9, 10, I John 2).

elper of the weak,

I give You praise and thanks for my children, for Your hands fashioned and made them. You clothed them with skin and flesh, and knit them together with bones and sinews. You have granted them life and steadfast love, and Your care has preserved their spirits.

Therefore please do not destroy them altogether. Remember that You have made them like clay, and do not return them to the dust. Are not their days few? Therefore please bless them, and do not fill them with disgrace. Work wonders *for them*, and not against them.

Oh, that You would speak and open Your lips to them, and that You would tell them the secrets of wisdom! For You are manifold in understanding.

Know, children, that God exacts of you less than your guilt deserves, because of Christ. He has taken your guilt upon Himself, therefore be of good cheer and rejoice in the abundant life given you in Him!

Thank You, Father, that because of Your Son, they can lift up their faces without blemish; they can be secure and not fear. Let their lives be brighter than the noonday, and their darkness like the morning. May they feel secure, because there is hope—hope in Jesus. Let them lie down with none to make them afraid. Amen (Job 10 & 11).

*Prayer is the most tangible expression of trust in God.*
~Jerry Bridges

reat God,

In whose hand is the life of every living thing and the breath of all mankind, with You are wisdom and might; You have counsel and understanding. Therefore, impart these things to my magnificent children. Lead them with strength and sound wisdom. Let the eyes of their hearts feast upon Your splendor. Let them brighten at the sight of Your justice, and with the vision of Your righteousness. For You overthrow the mighty. You uncover the deeps out of darkness and bring deep darkness to light. You make nations great, and You destroy them; You enlarge nations, and lead them away.

When Your majesty terrifies them, and the dread of You falls upon them, let them run to Christ. Even when I am a worthless physician in the day of their calamity, let them cling continually to Christ. And though You slay them, let them hope in You. Do not hide Your face or count them as Your enemies. Please do not frighten them or make them inherit the iniquities of their youth (Job 12 & 13).

---

*Prayer is the acknowledgment of God's sovereignty and of our dependence upon Him to act on our behalf. Prudence is the acknowledgment of our responsibility to use all legitimate means. We must not separate the two.* ~Jerry Bridges

ajestic and mighty LORD,

Make my children wise. Impart to them holy insight. And let them not do away with the fear of God, or hinder meditation before You. Keep their iniquity from teaching their mouths, and let them not choose the tongue of the crafty. Open their ears to listen to Your council, so that they do not limit wisdom to themselves.

Protect them from the one who is abominable and corrupt, the man who drinks injustice like water. Let not distress and anguish terrify them; may they not prevail against them, for they have not trusted in emptiness, deceiving themselves. Do not tear them with Your wrath or hate them, or gnash Your teeth at them. Neither give them up to the ungodly or cast them into the hands of the wicked. Please do not break them apart, or seize them by the neck and dash them to pieces, or set them up as Your target, surrounding them with Your archers. Do not break them with breach upon breach, or run upon them like a warrior. For even though they deserve all these things, spare them because of Christ; let them abide in Him.

My children, hope continually in Christ! Look to Him alone for your salvation. Even now, behold, your witness is in heaven, and He who testifies for you is on high. He argues your case with God, as a son of man does with his neighbor.

O Father we offer You praise and thanks for the advocate You have given us in Jesus! (Job 15 & 16).

estorer of the broken in spirit, Even when my children make their beds in darkness, when reproach is cast upon them, when You strip their glory from them, and set darkness upon their paths, when their relatives fail them, and close friends forget them, when their intimate friends abhor them and those whom they love turn against them, let them hope in Christ. For He lives, and has stood upon the earth, and they shall see Him for themselves. Their eyes shall behold Him! May they long for that day and not lose heart.

Because they are found in Christ, let my children dance. Let them sing to the tambourine and the lyre and rejoice to the sound of the pipe. May they spend their days in prosperity. Let them receive instruction from Your Son's mouth, and lay up His words in their hearts. Cause them to turn always to You so that they will be built up, and remove injustice far from their houses.

My children, if you lay gold in the dust, and gold of Ophir among the stones of the torrent bed, then the Almighty will be your gold and your precious silver. For then you will delight yourselves in the Almighty and lift up your faces to God.

When they pray to You, hear them, and make light to shine on their ways. Be exalted! For You deliver them even though they are not innocent, and will grant them cleanness of hands (Job 17, 19, 21, 22).

*Whether we like it or not, asking is the rule of the Kingdom.*
~Charles Spurgeon

ighteous Judge,

Thank You that Christ comes even to Your seat and lays the case of my children before You. He alone is the upright man who can argue on their behalf so that they are acquitted forever by their Judge.

Behold, You know the way that they take; when You have tried them, let them come out as gold. Make their feet hold fast to Your steps; keep them in Your way and do not let them turn aside. Let them never depart from the commandment of Your lips; may they treasure the words of Your mouth more than their portion of food.

You are unchangeable, and who can turn You back? What You desire, do so in them. Complete what You have appointed for them. Even if You must terrify them and make their hearts faint, let them hope in Your steadfast love. May they trust Your hand when thick darkness covers their faces. Amen (Job 23).

*An attitude of acceptance says that we trust God, that He loves us, and knows what is best for us. Acceptance does not mean that we do not pray for physical healing, or for the conception and birth of a little one to our marriage. We should indeed pray for those things, but we should pray in a trusting way. We should realize that, though God can do all things, for infinitely wise and loving reasons, He may not do that which we pray that He will do. How do we know how long to pray? As long as we can pray trustingly, with an attitude of acceptance of His will, we should pray as long as the desire remains.*
~Jerry Bridges

od of dominion,

Is there any number to Your armies? Upon whom does Your light not arise? Thank You, that because of Christ, my dear children are in the right before You. Be praised! For they who are born of woman have Him as their purity. His hand pierced the fleeing serpent, and by His spirit they have been made fair.

My children, adore and fear our God with me. He stretches out the north over the void and hangs the earth on nothing. The pillars of heaven tremble and are astounded at His rebuke. By His power He stilled the sea; by His understanding He shattered Rahab, the terror of the deep. Behold, these are but the outskirts of His ways, and how small a whisper do we hear of Him!

Father, as long as their breath is in them, and Your spirit is in their nostrils, keep their lips from speaking falsehood, and their tongues from uttering deceit. Let them hold fast to Christ's righteousness and not let it go.

Grant them wisdom. For You alone understand the way to it, and know its place. You said, "Behold, the fear of the Lord, that is wisdom, and to turn away from evil is understanding." Therefore increase their fear of You; let them turn away from evil and gain discerning hearts (Job 25-28).

ise Almighty,

Oh, that You might watch over my children, making Your lamp to shine upon their heads, so that by Your light they may walk through darkness. Let Your friendship be upon our house, and stay always with them.

Keep their family all around them; may their steps be washed with blessing, and cause the rock to pour out for them streams of oil. When the ear hears of them, let it call them blessed, and when the eye sees them, let it approve, because they deliver the poor who cry for help, and the fatherless who have none to help them.

May the blessings of those who are about to perish come upon them, and may they cause the widow's heart to sing for joy. Put righteousness on them and clothe them with it; make their justice like a robe and a turban.

Let them be eyes to the blind, feet to the lame, and fathers and mothers to the needy. Let them search out the cause of even the one whom they do not know. Use them to break the fangs of the unrighteous and make them drop their prey from their teeth (Job 29).

od of justice and righteousness,

Make my dear children wise. Fill them with understanding so that men and women will listen to them and wait and keep silence for their counsel—that they may wait for them as for the rain and open their mouths as for the spring rain.

Let them not despair when their souls are poured out within them, when days of affliction have taken hold of them. When they are cast into the mire, and have become like dust and ashes, let them cry to You for help, and answer them. Even when You seem to have turned cruel to them, may they hope in Your promise; may they wait for Your unfailing love. Let them be men and women who weep for those whose days are hard, and whose souls grieve for the needy.

Assist me to comfort them when evil comes; when they have waited for light, but darkness comes. Grant me wisdom and compassion to bear their turmoil with them; to encourage them when days of affliction come to meet them. Be merciful to them, for they have not walked with falsehood and their feet have not hastened to deceit (Job 30).

ajestic LORD,

Keep my marvelous children from making gold their trust or calling fine gold their confidence. Let them not rejoice only because their wealth is abundant or because their hand has found much. Guard their hearts from being secretly enticed to worship the shining splendor of what has been made, for that would be false to You. May they not rejoice at the ruin of the one who hates them, or exult when evil overtakes him. Let not their mouths sin by asking for his life with a curse.

Sanctify them so that they may be able to say that the sojourner has not lodged in the street, that they have opened their doors to the traveler, that they have withheld nothing that the poor desired, and have not caused the eyes of the widow to fail, that they have not left the fatherless hungry. Keep them from concealing their transgressions as others do by hiding iniquity in their bosoms.

My children, behold, I am toward God as you are; I too was pinched off from a piece of clay. Let us together cling to Christ as our righteousness, for He is pure, without transgression; He is clean, and there is no iniquity in Him (Job 31 & 33).

*Intercessory prayer is the purifying bath into which the individual and the fellowship must enter every day.*
~Dietrich Bonhoeffer

God, who is greater than man,
Let my children hope in Christ when their souls draw near the pit, when their lives approach those who bring death. When they pray to You, please accept them; may they see Your face with a shout of joy, as You restore to them their righteousness.

My children, sing with me before men and say, "I sinned and perverted what was right, and it was not repaid to me. The LORD has redeemed my soul from going down into the pit, and my life shall look upon the light."

Do all these things with them, O Father, to bring back their souls from the pit, that they may be lighted with the light of life.

Listen to me; hear my words and give ear to me. Please teach my children wisdom. Thank You that they do not drink up scoffing like water, that You have kept them from being men and women who travel in company with evildoers or walk with wicked men. May they never say, "It profits a man nothing that they should take delight in God," for such are the words of the wicked (Job 33 & 34).

*True, whole prayer is nothing but love.* ~St. Augustine

Father, perfect in knowledge, Be praised among the nations! For You have made my priceless children because You are mighty in strength and understanding. Do not despise them; when they are afflicted please give them their right and keep them alive. Do not withdraw Your eyes from them.

Open their ears to instruction and help them to return from iniquity. May they listen and serve You, and complete their days in prosperity, and their years in pleasantness. Let them not cherish anger as the godless in heart. Deliver them by their affliction and open their ears by adversity. Allure them out of distress into a broad place, and may what is set on their table be full of fatness.

My children, behold, God is exalted in His power; who is a teacher like Him? Who has prescribed for Him His way, or who can say, "You have done wrong?" Remember to extol His work, of which men have sung. Behold, God is great, and we know Him not, the number of His years is unsearchable. For He draws up the drops of water; they distill His mist in rain which the skies pour down and drop on mankind abundantly. Can anyone understand the spreading of the clouds, the thunderings of His pavilion? Behold, He scatters His lightning about Him and covers the roots of the sea. For by these He judges peoples; He gives food in abundance. He covers His hands with the lightning and commands it to strike the mark. Its crashing declares His presence; the cattle also declare that He rises (Job 36).

od of thunderous majesty, Let my lovely children sing of Your power; when they see it let their hearts tremble and leap out of their place. For You thunder wondrously with Your voice; You do great things that we cannot comprehend. May they bow before You when they behold the strength of Your word, for to the snow You say, "Fall on the earth," likewise to the downpour, Your mighty downpour. May they worship You with reverent hearts, for by Your breath ice is given, and the broad waters are frozen fast. Let their hearts tremble before You in wonder, for You load the thick cloud with moisture; the clouds scatter Your lightning. They turn around and around by Your guidance, to accomplish all that You command them on the face of the habitable world. Whether for correction or for Your land or for love, You cause it to happen.

Hear me, my children; stop and consider the wondrous works of God.

LORD, I praise You, for they indeed are some of Your most wondrous works—more amazing than the rain, the lightning, the wind, or the clouds; they shine and declare the glory of Him who is perfect in knowledge.

May they worship You as they look on the light when it is bright in the skies, when the wind has passed and cleared them. Out of the north comes golden splendor; You are clothed with awesome majesty. Let them praise You as the One great in power, in justice, and abundant in righteousness. Therefore, let them fear You. Amen (Job 37).

ather of my Lord Jesus Christ,

According to Your foreknowledge, in the sanctification of the Spirit, for obedience to Jesus Christ and for sprinkling with His blood: may grace and peace be multiplied to my wonderful children.

Let them bless You, for according to Your great mercy, You have caused them to be born again to a living hope through the resurrection of Jesus Christ from the dead, to an inheritance that is imperishable, undefiled, and unfading, kept in heaven for them. Thank You that by Your power they are being guarded through faith for a salvation ready to be revealed in the last time. Let them rejoice in this. May they rejoice even when it is necessary that they be grieved for a little while by various trials, so that the tested genuineness of their faith—more precious than gold that perishes though it is tested by fire—may be found to result in praise and glory and honor at the revelation of Jesus Christ. Though they have not seen Him, let them love Him all the more. Though they do not now see Him, I praise You that they believe in Him and rejoice with joy that is inexpressible and filled with glory, obtaining the outcome of their faith, the salvation of their souls (I Peter 1).

*Prayer does not fit us for the greater work,*
*prayer is the greater work.* ~Oswald Chambers

ather of our living hope,

O that You would assist my children to prepare their minds for action, and to be sober-minded. Let them set their hope fully on the grace that will be brought at the revelation of Jesus Christ. As obedient children, may they not be conformed to the passions of their former ignorance. Instead, as You who called them are holy, make them holy in all their conduct, since it is written, "You shall be holy, for I am holy." And since You are their Father who judges impartially according to their deeds, cause them to conduct themselves with fear throughout the time of their exile on this earth, knowing that they were ransomed from the futile ways inherited from their forefathers, not with perishable things such as silver or gold, but with the precious blood of Christ, like that of a lamb without blemish or spot.

My children, He was made manifest in the last times for your sake, for through Him you are believers in God, who raised Him from the dead and gave Him glory, so that your faith and hope are in God.

Enable us, O LORD, to purify our souls by our obedience to the truth for a sincere love, so that we may love one another earnestly from a pure heart, since we have been born again, not of perishable seed but of imperishable, through Your living and abiding word. Praise be to Your name! For this word is the good news that was preached to us. Amen (I Peter 1).

ternal LORD,

By Your mighty Spirit enable my children to put away all malice and all deceit and hypocrisy and envy and all slander. Make them long for the pure spiritual milk, that by it they may grow up to salvation—since indeed they have tasted that You are good.

Thank You that as they come to Christ, a living stone rejected by men but in Your sight chosen and precious, they are being built up like living stones into a spiritual house to be part of a holy priesthood, to offer spiritual sacrifices acceptable to You through Jesus Christ.

I praise You that they are part of Your chosen race, Your royal priesthood, Your holy nation, and a people for Your own possession. And because they are, let them ever proclaim Your excellencies—for You are the God who has called them out of darkness into Your marvelous light. Thank You that although they once were not of a people, now they are of Your people; once they had not received mercy, but now they have received mercy.

Children, I urge you as sojourners and exiles to abstain from the passions of the flesh, which wage war against your souls.

Father, keep their conduct among the Gentiles honorable, so that when they speak against them as evildoers, they may see their good deeds and glorify You on the day of visitation (I Peter 2).

*To clasp the hands in prayer is the beginning of an uprising against the disorder of the world.* ~Karl Barth

ORD of unbounded mercy,

Help my children to live as those who are free, not using their freedom as a cover-up for evil, but living as Your bondservants. Let them honor everyone, love the brotherhood, fear You, and honor the governing authorities.

Grant them the grace to endure sorrows while suffering unjustly, being mindful of You. For if when they do good and suffer for it they endure, this is a gracious thing in Your sight.

For to this you have been called, my children, because Christ also suffered for you leaving an example, so that you might follow in His steps. He committed no sin, neither was deceit found in His mouth.

O God, make them like Him, so that when they are reviled, they will not revile in return. When they suffer, let them not threaten, but continue entrusting themselves to You who judge justly. Thank You that we have a perfect example in Christ Jesus! He himself bore our sins in His body on the tree, that we might die to sin and live to righteousness. May He be exalted! For by His wounds we have been healed. Thank You, that even though they were straying like sheep, now they have returned to You, the Shepherd and Overseer of their souls. Amen (I Peter 2).

ou who have called us to
Your eternal glory in Christ,
Do not let my children repay evil for evil or reviling for reviling, but on the contrary, may they bless, for to this they were called, that they may obtain a blessing. I desire them to love life and see good days, therefore keep their tongues from evil and their lips from speaking deceit; let them turn away from evil and do good; let them seek peace and pursue it. For Your eyes are on the righteous, and Your ears are open to their prayer. But Your face is against those who do evil.

My children, even if you should suffer for righteousness' sake, you will be blessed. Rejoice, and have no fear of man, nor be troubled.

Father, may they regard Christ the Lord as holy in their hearts, and always be prepared to make a defense to anyone who asks them for a reason for the hope that is in them. Let them do it with gentleness and respect, having a good conscience, so that, when they are slandered, those who revile their good behavior in Christ may be put to shame (I Peter 3).

*God delights in the aroma of his own glory
as he smells it in the prayers of his people.* ~John Piper

od of all Grace,

If my children are insulted for the name of Christ, let them take comfort in the truth that they are blessed, because the Spirit of glory and of God rests upon them. If they suffer as Christians, let them not be ashamed, but let them glorify You in that name. Indeed, when they suffer according to Your will, let them entrust their souls to You—their faithful Creator—while doing good.

Children, do not be surprised at the fiery trial when it comes upon you to test you, as though something strange were happening to you. But rejoice insofar as you share Christ's sufferings, that you may also rejoice and be glad when His glory is revealed.

Father, help me to shepherd these priceless children with whom You have entrusted me, not under compulsion, but eagerly and joyfully, as You would have me; not domineering over them, but being an example. Please clothe them with humility toward one another, for You oppose the proud but give grace to the humble. We want *You*. We need Your grace. Humble us, therefore, under Your mighty hand so that at the proper time You may exalt us. We cast our anxieties on You, because You care for us. Make us sober-minded. May they be watchful. Enable them to resist our adversary the devil firm in their faith, and remind them that the same kinds of suffering are being experienced by their brotherhood throughout the world. And when they have suffered a little while, restore, confirm, strengthen, and establish them. To You be the dominion forever and ever. Amen (I Peter 4 & 5).

ompassionate Father,
May grace and peace be multiplied to my children in the knowledge of You and of Jesus our Lord. Thank You that Your divine power has granted to them all things that pertain to life and godliness, through the knowledge of You who called us to Your own glory and excellence, by which You have granted to them Your precious and very great promises, so that through them they may become partakers of the divine nature, having escaped from the corruption that is in the world because of sinful desire.

Because of this great blessing, help them to make every effort to supplement their faith with virtue, and virtue with knowledge, and knowledge with self-control, and self-control with steadfastness, and steadfastness with godliness, and godliness with brotherly affection, and brotherly affection with love. Make these qualities their own and let them increase in them, to keep them from being ineffective or unfruitful in the knowledge of our Lord Jesus Christ. May they never be so nearsighted that they are blind, forgetting that they were cleansed from their former sins. Therefore, assist them to be all the more diligent to make their calling and election sure, for if they practice these qualities they will never fall. Please uphold them! And richly provide for them an entrance into the eternal kingdom of our Lord and Savior Jesus Christ. Hasten the coming of His kingdom, I pray (II Peter 1).

*Prayer is the power that wields the weapon of the Word; but the Word itself is the weapon by which the nations will be brought to faith and obedience.* ~John Piper

aithful King,

Make my children the sort of men and women who live lives of holiness and godliness, waiting for and hastening the coming of the day of God, because of which the heavens will be set on fire and dissolved, and the heavenly bodies will melt as they burn. While we wait for a new heavens and a new earth in which righteousness dwells, let them be diligent to be found by You without spot or blemish, and at peace.

Protect them from false teachers that will rise up and secretly bring destructive heresies. Let them not be found among the many who will follow their sensuality and blaspheme the way of truth. Keep them far from the way of the unrighteous, who speak loud boasts of folly and are slaves to corruption. May it never be that after they have escaped the defilements of the world through the knowledge of our Lord and Savior Jesus Christ, they are again entangled in them and overcome! Guard them from such a fate, for their last state would become worse for them than the first.

Therefore, children, take care that you are not carried away with the error of lawless people and lose your own stability. But grow in the grace and knowledge of our Lord and Savior Jesus Christ.

Father, may they grow in such grace and knowledge! To You be the glory both now and to the day of eternity. Amen (II Peter 2 & 3).

ather,

Let whatever happens to my children serve to advance the gospel, so that even their suffering and imprisonment may magnify Christ. May their lives be a source of confidence for others in You, that makes them much more bold to speak the word without fear.

Keep them from proclaiming Christ out of envy or rivalry, and instead let them do so from good will and out of love. More than that, let them rejoice in Christ, and in His truth proclaimed. And help them to continue stirring up others for their progress and joy in the faith.

Please let their manner of life be worthy of the gospel of Christ, so that we may stand firm in one spirit, with one mind striving side by side for the faith of the gospel, and not frightened in anything by our opponents. Thank you that it has been granted to us that for the sake of Christ we should not only believe in Him but also suffer for His sake.

Fill them with the joy of being of the same mind, having the same love, being in full accord and of one mind. Keep them from doing anything from rivalry or conceit, but let them in humility count others more significant than themselves. Let each of them look not only to their own interests, but also to the interests of others, having the very mind of Christ (Philippians 1 & 2).

*The true theology is warm, and it steams upward into prayer.*
~P.T. Forsyth

ighly exalted God,

Please grow my children into men and women who do all things without grumbling or questioning, that they may be blameless and innocent, children of God without blemish in the midst of a crooked and twisted generation. Let them shine as lights in the world, holding fast to the word of life, so that in the day of Christ I may be proud that I did not pray in vain or encourage them in vain. Enable me to rejoice and be glad to suffer for their sake—even to pour out my life as a drink offering upon the sacrificial offering of their faith. Likewise let them also be glad and rejoice with me to endure hardship for the name of Christ. Make them genuinely concerned for the welfare of others, seeking not their own interests but those of Jesus Christ.

My children, rejoice in the Lord. To say this same thing to you is no trouble to me and is safe for you. Look out for the dogs, look out for the evildoers, look out for those who put confidence in their works.

Father, help them to remain steadfast in worship by Your Spirit, glorying in Christ Jesus, and putting no confidence in the flesh. More than anything, strengthen them to forget what lies behind and strain forward to what lies ahead, and press on toward the goal for the prize of Your upward call in Christ Jesus. Let them also hold true to what they have attained. Amen (Philippians 2 & 3).

reat Savior,

Thank you that my children's citizenship is in heaven! Therefore let them not set their minds on earthly things, but instead await a Savior, the Lord Jesus Christ, who will transform their lowly bodies to be like His glorious body, by the power that enables Him even to subject all things to Himself.

Therefore my children, whom I love and long for, my joy and crown, stand firm in the Lord. Rejoice in the Lord always; again I will say, Rejoice!

Father, teach them how to be content in every situation. Help them to know how to be brought low, and how to abound. In any and every circumstance show them the secret of facing plenty and hunger, abundance and need. Strengthen them to do all things through You. Please supply every need of theirs according to Your riches in glory in Christ Jesus. To You, our God and Father, be glory forever and ever! May the grace of the Lord Jesus Christ be with their spirits. Amen (Philippians 3 & 4).

*When you encounter trial and suffering, what's the content of your prayer? If yours is primarily a plea for relief from suffering, then please know that this is biblical. It's certainly not unbiblical. We're encouraged by God in Scripture to pray for relief from suffering. But this should never be the exclusive focus of our prayers in those times.* ~C.J. Mahaney

overeign LORD of Zion,
Let my children sing aloud and shout! May they rejoice and exult with all their hearts, for You have taken away the judgments against them because of Christ. You have cleared away their enemies—death, sin, and Satan. Let them never again fear evil, for You—the King of Israel, the LORD—are near them.

May they not fear, and let not their hands grow weak.

O children of Zion, the LORD your God is with you, a mighty one who will save; He rejoices over you with gladness; He quiets you by His love; He exults over You with loud singing.

LORD God, when they mourn, please gather them and bring them to Your festival, so that they will no longer suffer reproach. Deal with all their oppressors. Change their shame into praise and renown in all the earth. Restore their fortunes so that You will be renowned and praised among all the peoples of the earth (Zephaniah 3).

*Restraining pray'r, we cease to fight;*
*Pray'r makes the Christian's armour bright.*
~William Cowper

od our Savior,

Thank You for Christ Jesus our hope. Watch over my children and guard them from those who teach any different doctrine, or devote themselves to myths, who promote speculations rather than the good order from You that is by faith. And as you protect them, fill them with the love that issues from a pure heart and a good conscience and a sincere faith. Let them not swerve from these, or wander away into vain discussion.

I thank You, Christ Jesus my Lord, for giving them strength, and because You judged them faithful, appointing them to Your service, though formerly they were so unworthy.

My children, rejoice! Remember that you received mercy, and the grace of our Lord overflowed for you with the faith and love that are in Christ Jesus.

I praise You, Father, for showing them mercy, so that in them Jesus Christ might display His perfect patience as an example to those who are to believe in Him for eternal life.

To You, the King of ages, immortal, invisible, the only God, be honor and glory forever and ever! Amen (I Timothy 1).

*There is nothing so abnormal, so unworldly, so supernatural, in human life as prayer.... The whole Christian life in so far as it is lived from the Cross and by the Cross is rationally an extravagance. ~P.T. Forsyth*

ighty LORD,

I entrust my children entirely to Your charge and care, in accordance with Your grace in Christ Jesus toward them. By Your power may they wage the good warfare, holding faith and a good conscience. Let them never make shipwreck of their faith!

Help me to be a parent who prays without anger or quarreling. Give my daughters the wisdom and desire to adorn themselves in respectable apparel, with modesty and self-control, not merely with braided hair and gold or pearls or costly attire, but with what is proper for women who profess godliness—with good works. Let them be the kind of women who learn quietly with all submissiveness.

Protect my children from those who depart from the faith by devoting themselves to deceitful spirits and teachings of demons. Let them have nothing to do with irreverent, silly myths. Rather train them for godliness, for while bodily training is of some value, godliness is of value in every way, as it holds promise for the present life and also for the life to come.

May they toil and strive to this end, because they have their hope set on You, the living God (I Timothy 1, 2, 4).

*If we do not abide in prayer,*
*we shall abide in cursed temptations.* ~John Owen

avior of the weak,

Let my precious children set an example for believers in speech, in conduct, in love, in faith, in purity.

Make them find full delight in the sound words of our Lord Jesus Christ and the teaching that accords with godliness. And keep them from an unhealthy craving for controversy and for quarrels about words. Let them instead pursue godliness with contentment, for therein there is great gain.

May they be content that they have food and clothing, and let them not desire to be rich.

My children, let me remind you that those who desire to be rich fall into temptation, into a snare, into many senseless and harmful desires that plunge people into ruin and destruction.

Father, guard them from craving riches! For the love of money is the root of all kinds of evils. Keep them from the fate of those who, through this craving, have wandered away from the faith and pierced themselves with many pangs.

Let their love and craving be for Christ (I Timothy 4 & 6).

*For, as for my heart, when I go to pray, I find it so loth to go to God, and when it is with him, so loth to stay with him, that many times I am forced in my Prayers; first to beg God that he would take mine heart, and set it on himself in Christ, and when it is there, that he would keep it there (Psalm 86.11).*
~John Bunyan

ather of glory,

As for my children, let them flee from the desire to be rich and the love of money. Help and enable them to pursue with renewed vigor righteousness, godliness, faith, love, steadfastness, and gentleness. Strengthen them to fight the good fight of the faith, and to take hold of the eternal life to which they were called.

My children, I charge you in the presence of God, who gives life to all things, and of Christ Jesus, to keep your conduct unstained and free from reproach until the appearing of our Lord Jesus Christ, which He will display at the proper time—He who is the blessed and only Sovereign, the King of kings and Lord of lords, who alone has immortality, who dwells in unapproachable light, whom no one has ever seen or can see.

To You, O God, be honor and eternal dominion! If You bless them with plenty, let them never become haughty or set their hopes on the uncertainty of riches. Rather cause them to set their hopes on You—the One who richly provides them with everything to enjoy. Help them to do good, to be rich in good works, to be generous and ready to share, thus storing up treasure for themselves as a good foundation for the future so that they may take hold of that which is truly life (I Timothy 6).

od and Father,

May grace, mercy, and peace be multiplied to my dearest children. I thank You as I remember them constantly in my prayers night and day. Thank You for granting me children who fill me with joy with each new sight of them. Please grow their faith in sincerity. Fan into flame the gifts You have given them, and remind them that You gave us a spirit not of fear but of power and love and self-control.

Therefore let them not be ashamed of the testimony about our Lord, but by Your power cause them to rejoice to share in suffering for the gospel. For You are the one who saved them and called them to a holy calling, not because of their works but because of Your own purpose and grace, which You gave them in Christ Jesus before the ages began. Thank You that He is their Savior, even He who abolished death and brought life and immortality to light through the gospel. Let them not be ashamed to suffer for this gospel, for they know whom they have believed.

My children, follow the pattern of the sound words that you have heard from the Scriptures, in the faith and love that are in Christ Jesus. By the Holy Spirit who dwells within us, guard the good deposit entrusted to you (II Timothy 1).

*It is not well for a man to pray cream and live skim milk.*
~Henry Ward Beecher

ather in heaven,

Please strengthen my children by the grace that is in Christ Jesus, so that they may be able to share in suffering as His good soldiers. May they constantly remember Jesus Christ, risen from the dead, the offspring of David. Let them rejoice to endure everything for the sake of the elect, that they also may obtain the salvation that is in Christ Jesus with eternal glory.

My children, the saying is trustworthy, for: If we have died with Him, we will also live with Him; if we endure, we will also reign with Him; if we deny Him, He also will deny us; if we are faithless, He remains faithful—for He cannot deny Himself.

O God, remind them of these things. Compel them to do their best to present themselves to You as ones approved, workers who have no need to be ashamed, rightly handling the word of truth. May they avoid irreverent babble, for it will lead people into more and more ungodliness, and their talk will spread like gangrene. Thank You that Your firm foundation stands, bearing this seal: "The Lord knows those who are His," and "Let everyone who names the name of the Lord depart from iniquity" (II Timothy 2).

---

*Were it not for the Spirit, none would be able to persevere in prayer. 'A man without the help of the Spirit', John Bunyan once declared, 'cannot so much as pray once; much less, continue...in a sweet praying frame.' It needs to be noted that, for all who persevere in this struggle and discipline of prayer, there are times of exquisite delight when the struggle, and duty slides over into pure joy.* ~Michael A. G. Haykin

oly Master,

Let my dear children cleanse themselves from what is dishonorable so that they will be vessels for honorable use, set apart as holy, useful to You, ready for every good work.

Make them flee youthful passions and pursue righteousness, faith, love, and peace, along with those who call on the Lord from a pure heart. May they have nothing to do with foolish, ignorant controversies, since they breed quarrels. Let them not be quarrelsome but kind to everyone.

Help them to patiently endure evil. Protect them from those who are lovers of self, lovers of money, proud, arrogant, abusive, disobedient to their parents, ungrateful, unholy, heartless, unappeasable, slanderous, without self-control, brutal, not loving good, treacherous, reckless, swollen with conceit, lovers of pleasure rather than lovers of You, having the appearance of godliness, but denying its power. Help them to avoid such people.

Enable me to lead them righteously in my teaching, my conduct, my aim in life, my faith, my patience, my love, my steadfastness, and my persecutions and sufferings.

Indeed, children, let me remind you that all who desire to live a godly life in Christ Jesus will be persecuted, while evil people and imposters will go on from bad to worse, deceiving and being deceived.

But as for them, Lord God, may they continue in what they have learned and have firmly believed, becoming more and more acquainted with the sacred writings, which are able to make them wise for salvation through faith in Christ Jesus. Increase their love for Scripture. May what You have breathed out teach them, reprove them, correct them, and train them in righteousness, that they may be competent, equipped for every good work (II Timothy 2 & 3).

*My simple exhortation is this: Let us take time this very day to rethink our priorities and how prayer fits in. Make some new resolve. Try some new venture with God. Set a time. Set a place. Choose a portion of Scripture to guide you. Don't be tyrannized by the press of busy days. We all need midcourse corrections. Make this a day of turning to prayer—for the glory of God and for the fullness of your joy.*
~John Piper

od and Father of Christ Jesus,
who is to judge the living and the dead,
May my incomparable children delight in and spread Your word all the more. Make them ready to bear witness to Christ's appearing and His kingdom in season and out of season. Let them reprove, rebuke, and exhort their brothers and sisters in Christ with complete patience and teaching.

Guard them from becoming men and women who will not endure sound teaching—ones who, having itching ears, accumulate for themselves teachers to suit their own passions, and turn away from listening to the truth and wander off into myths. May it never be! Instead, keep them always sober-minded. Enable them to endure suffering, to do the work of an evangelist, and to fulfill the ministry to which You have called them.

O Father, please strengthen them to fight the good fight. Carry them onward to finish the race. Keep them so that they might keep the faith. Effect their hearts to love Christ's appearing all the more, so that there may be laid up for them the crown of righteousness, which He, the righteous judge, will award to them on that Day.

May Christ Jesus and His grace be with their spirits. Amen (II Timothy 4).

*May God give us a heart and a will to make prayer, prayer for the exaltation of God and extension of the kingdom, a daily reality in our lives.* ~Michael A. G. Haykin

# Appendix A

## Books Quoted

Bounds, E.M. *Man of Prayer*

Bridges, Jerry. *Trusting God: Even When Life Hurts*

Brother Lawrence. *The Practice of the Presence of God*

Buttrick, George A. *Prayer*

Carson, D.A. *Call to Spiritual Reformation: Priorities from Paul and His Prayers*

Di Gangi, Marioano. *A Golden Treasury of Puritan Devotions*

Dubay, Thomas. *The Evidential Power of Beauty*

Edwards, Jonathan. *Religious Affections*

Edwards, Jonathan. *The Works of Jonathan Edwards, Vol. 2*

Forsyth, P.T. *The Soul of Prayer*

Grudem, Wayne. *Systematic Theology*

Haykin, Michael. *The God Who Draws Near*

Hosier, Helen. *Jonathan Edwards: The Great Awakener*

Mahaney, C.J. *Humility: True Greatness*

Mason, Mike. *Champagne for the Soul*

Mason, Mike. *Practicing the Presence of People*

Mason, Mike. *The Gospel According to Job*

Mason, Mike. *The Mystery of Marriage*

Merton, Thomas. *Contemplative Prayer*

Montgomery, L.M. *Emily Climbs*

Montgomery, L.M. *The Story Girl*

Mueller, George. *Autobiography of George Mueller*

Murray, Ian. *Jonathan Edwards: A New Biography*

Owen, John. *The Glory of Christ*

Packer, J.I. *Evangelism and the Sovereignty of God*

Piper, John, and Justin Taylor. *A God Entranced Vision of All Things*

Piper, John. *A Hunger for God: Desiring God Through Fasting and Prayer*

Piper, John. *Pierced by the Word*

Piper, John. *The Pleasures of God*

Piper, John. *The Roots of Endurance*

Piper, John. *What Jesus Demands from the World*

Spurgeon, Charles. *Lectures to My Students*

Spurgeon, Charles. *The Soul Winner*

Torrey, R.A. *How to Pray*

Tozer, A. W. *God Tells the Man Who Cares*

Ware, Bruce. *God's Greater Glory*

Whitney, Donald. *Spiritual Disciplines for the Christian Life*

Whyte, Alexander. *Lord Teach Us to Pray*

## For Further Reading on the Subject of Prayer

Bennett, Arthur. *The Valley of Vision: Puritan Prayers and Devotions*

Calvin, John. *The Institutes of Christian Religion* (Book 3)

Carson, D.A. *Teach Us to Pray: Prayer in the Bible and the World*

Henry, Matthew. *A Method for Prayer*

Hunter, W. Bingham. *The God Who Hears*

Owen, John. *Communion With God*

Palmer, B.M. *Theology of Prayer*

Piper, John. *Desiring God* (Chapter 6)

Piper, John. *When I Don't Desire God: How to Fight for Joy*

Pratt, Jr. Richard L. *Pray With Your Eyes Open*

Spurgeon, Charles. *Prayer and Spiritual Warfare*

Whitney, Donald. *Spiritual Disciplines for the Christian Life*

## For Further Reading on the Subject of Parenting

Baucham, Voddie. *Family Driven Faith*

Brandt, Carol. *Old Paths for Little Feet*

Castleman, Robbie and Ruth Graham. *Parenting in the Pew: Guiding Your Children into the Joy of Worship*

Clarkson, Sally. *The Mission of Motherhood: Touching Your Child's Heart for Eternity*

Durbin, Kara. *Parenting With Scripture: A Topical Guide for Teachable Moments*

Fleming, Jean. *A Mother's Heart: A* Look *at Values, Vision, and Character for the Christian Mother*

Jones, M.L. *Raising Children God's Way*

Mally, Sarah and Stephen Mally, et al. *Making Brothers and Sisters Best Friends*

Maxwell, Steven. *Keeping Our Children's Hearts: Our Vital Priority*

Rosemond, John. *Parenting by the Book*

Sande, Ken. *Peacemaking for Families*

Starr, Meade. *Training Hearts, Teaching Minds: Family Devotions Based on the Shorter Catechism*

Thomas, Gary. *Sacred Parenting*

Tripp, Paul. *Age of Opportunity: A Biblical Guide to Parenting Teens*

Tripp, Tedd. *Shepherding a Child's Heart*

Ware, Bruce. *Big Truths for Young Hearts: Teaching and Learning the Greatness of God*

Whitney, Donald. *Family Worship*

# Appendix B
## Prayers by Biblical Book & Chapter

# Also available from Andrew Case:

*Water of the Word:*
*Intercession for Her*

*Prayers of an*
*Excellent Wife*

These books do *not* exist to make money. They exist to edify the Church, spread and deepen a passion for Scripture, and adorn the Gospel. This is why we offer them for free online and sell them for as little as possible. If anyone simply cannot afford to pay for these books, there is a Whatever-You-Can-Afford policy. We will accept whatever you're able to pay—even if it's nothing. It is our joy and delight to give freely what has been freely given to us (Matthew 10:8). We never want to make cost "an obstacle in the way of the gospel of Christ" (I Corinthians 9:12). So if you'd like a copy of a book, but your limited cash-flow prevents it, don't be ashamed! Just contact us and let us know what you'd like, and it will be our pleasure to fill your request.

Phone: 502-802-4383          Email: andrewdcase@gmail.com

Download *Water of the Word, Prayers of an Excellent Wife,* or *Setting Their Hope in GOD* (as PDF) online for free at:
**www.HisMagnificence.com**

**4HM3HHEE** Use this coupon code to order *Water of the Word, Prayers of an Excellent Wife,* or this book for less than $5 per copy. Go to HisMagnificence.com and click on "Books", and there will be links on that page which will direct you to the store where you can use the coupon code. It does not expire and has no quantity limits.

## Upcoming titles from Andrew Case:

*Prayers of an Excellent Wife* (Spanish)
    Anticipated release date: Summer 2010